Best Short Hikes
In and Around
the North Sacramento Valley

Best Short Hikes
In and Around
the North Sacramento Valley

• • • • • • • • • • • • •

BY JOHN R. SOARES

THE
MOUNTAINEERS

9 8 7 6 5
5 4 3 2

Published by The Mountaineers
1011 SW Klickitat Way, Seattle, Washington 98134

Published simultaneously in Canada by Douglas & McIntyre,
Ltd., 1615 Venables Street, Vancouver, B.C. V5L 2H1

Published simultaneously in Great Britain by Cordee, 3a
DeMontfort Street, Leicester, England, LE1 7HD

Manufactured in the United States of America

Edited by Carolyn Threadgill
Maps by Helen Sherman
Cover design by Elizabeth Watson
Book layout by Barbara Bash
All photographs by John R. Soares except as indicated

Cover photograph: Castle Dome and Mount Shasta, by Rick Ramos
Frontispiece: A hiker cools her feet in the clear waters of Mill Creek near Whiskeytown Lake.

Library of Congress Cataloging in Publication Data

Soares, John R.
    Best short hikes in and around the north Sacramento Valley / by
John Soares.
        p.   cm.
    Includes bibliographical references (p.   ) and index.
    ISBN 0-89886-318-X
    1. Hiking—California—Sacramento River Valley—Guide-books.
    2. Sacramento River Valley (Calif.)—Description and travel—Guide
    -books.   I. Title.
    GV199.42.C22S237   1992   91-39987
    917.94′5—dc20   CIP

*I dedicate this book to my father, John Severin Soares,
who taught me to love and respect nature*

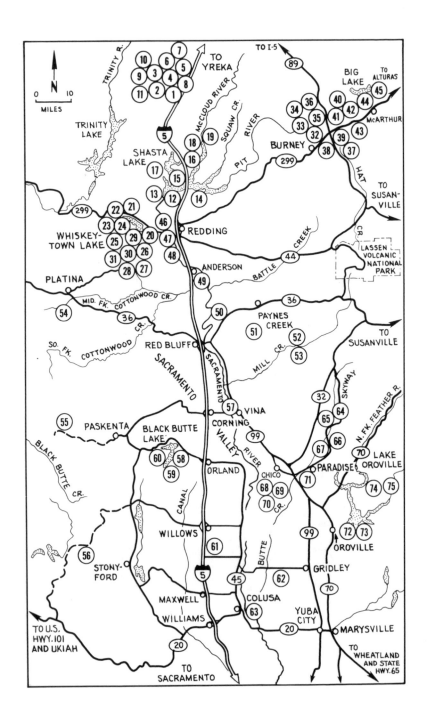

6

Contents

· · · · · · · · · · ·

Acknowledgments

For their pleasant companionship and encouragement, I thank the good friends who hiked many of the trails with me: Rick Ramos, Greg Haling, my brother Marc Soares, and my sister Camille Soares. I owe special gratitude to Kathy Hansen, who read the entire manuscript and made many valuable suggestions. In addition, Sharyn Cornelius, Ken Daniels, Ginger Bristow, and Pamela Baker Heighet read sections of the manuscript, and their honest input was invaluable. I also wish to acknowledge the many people who graciously answered my phone queries and read drafts for the hikes under their jurisdiction. Several were especially helpful: Isobel Krell of the Castle Crag Interpretive Association, Peter Kola of the Shasta-Trinity National Forest, Carl Turner of the Shasta Lake National Recreation Area, Chuck Heackok of the Whiskeytown National Recreation Area, and Joe Williams of the Bureau of Land Management. Finally, I thank The Mountaineers Books staff for their guidance and diligence.

INTRODUCTION

· · · · · · · · · · ·

The North Sacramento Valley

The Sacramento Valley and its surrounding hills and mountains contain a diversity of natural regions: lush riparian habitat lines the banks of the Sacramento River, dense stands of pine and fir hug steep mountainsides, and stunted pines eke out a lonely existence on high, weather-beaten ridges.

This book, your guide to exploring these areas on foot, offers comprehensive coverage of day hikes in the Sacramento Valley north of Sacramento, and nearly all day hikes in the bordering hills and mountains within an hour's drive of the valley. Castle Crags State Park, Shasta Lake National Recreation Area, Whiskeytown National Recreation Area, and McArthur–Burney Falls State Park receive extra attention because they offer extensive hiking and other recreational opportunities.

All trails in this book combine walking with the opportunity to observe nature. On some trails, such as those in and near Redding and Chico,

The author surveys Shasta Lake and the surrounding oak- and pine-clad mountains from the Overlook Trail (hike 15). (photo by Rick Ramos)

you'll occasionally encounter the sights and sounds of civilization. Other trails take you deep into unsullied wilderness and allow complete solitude.

The day hikes range in length from 0.5 mile to more than 13 miles. Some are ideally suited for the family with young children; others will challenge even the most fit. Regardless of your age and ability, you'll find numerous trails that suit you.

REGIONAL GEOGRAPHY

Hikes covered in this book lie in five geographical areas: the Klamath Mountains, which include Castle Crags, Shasta Lake, and Whiskeytown Lake; the Cascades, which include Burney Falls, Hat Creek, and the Pit River; the Coast Range on the Sacramento Valley's west side, which includes Snow Mountain and Mount Linn; the Sierra Nevada, which includes the area around Paradise and east of Oroville; and the Sacramento Valley itself, which includes the valley floor and the hills between Red Bluff and Redding.

REGIONAL HISTORY

Native American tribes, such as the Wintu, Ahjumawi, and Yana, were the first inhabitants of the Sacramento Valley and its surrounding hills and mountains. White settlers arrived in the area in the mid-1840s, and thousands of prospectors soon followed during the Gold Rush. By the late nineteenth century, timber companies had begun harvesting ponderosa pine and Douglas fir in the mountains, and farmers were turning the Sacramento Valley into one of the most productive agricultural regions in the world. Recent years have witnessed a dramatic population increase as residents of Los Angeles and the San Francisco Bay Area have been lured to Chico, Redding, and the smaller surrounding communities by the more relaxed lifestyle and spectacular natural beauty of the region.

NATURAL HISTORY

This section gives only a brief introduction to the complex and multifaceted subject of natural history. The reference section lists books that provide more detailed information. Also, the hike descriptions often discuss various aspects of trailside natural history in depth.

Plants. The best way to learn how to recognize major plant species is by hiking interpretive nature trails with an identification book in hand. These trails have either signs or numbered posts with an accompanying brochure, and allow you to identify the plant and note its important characteristics. Nature trails included in this book are the Indian Creek Trail (hike 1) at Castle Crags, the Davis Gulch (hike 29) and Shasta Divide (hike 20) trails at Whiskeytown Lake, the Falls Trail (hike 32) at McArthur–Burney Falls State Park, the Big Oak (hike 59) and Buckhorn (hike 60) trails at Black Butte Lake, the trails at Bille Park (hike 67) and the Upper Ridge Nature Park (hike 66) near Paradise, and the Chaparral Trail (hike 72) at Lake Oroville. Also, local naturalists often lead nature walks. This is another excellent way to learn about plants and other interesting aspects of natural history. (Check local newspapers and nature centers for dates and times of nature walks.)

Botanists use the concept of "plant community" to help categorize different plants that tend to grow in similar habitats. Elevation is most important in discerning plant communities, but soil characteristics, amount of available water, and local variations in temperature and sunlight exposure are also relevant.

Different plant communities can exist at the same elevation. This is especially apparent from 1,000 to 3,000 feet, where one often sees foothill woodland plants on a mountain's sunnier, drier, south side, and ponderosa-pine forest plants at the same elevation on the shadier, moister, north side.

The major plant communities are as follows:

Riparian Communities (various elevations). The roots of riparian plants can tolerate water-saturated soil; thus riparian communities are usually located next to standing or flowing water. Common trees and shrubs are cottonwoods, alders, sycamores, ailanthus, black locust, and willows. Ferns, horsetails, cattails, and various rushes, sedges, and grasses also grow in wet areas.

Central Valley (50–400 feet). The Central Valley includes land that generally has deep, relatively rich soil. Perennial grasses such as wild oats have largely been replaced by annuals brought in by settlers. Common tree species include valley oak, Fremont's cottonwood, and California sycamore. Several willow species grow in moist areas, along with nonnative trees such as ailanthus and black locust.

Foothill Woodland (500–3,000 feet). This plant community includes all the hills bordering the Sacramento Valley, and the lower mountain slopes. Digger pines, with their multiple crowns and bizarrely twisted trunks, stand out as the most prominent tree. A relatively uncommon tree, the diminutive buckeye, dots the landscape in certain areas. There are two species of oak: the deciduous blue oak and the evergreen interior live oak. The ubiquitous whiteleaf manzanita and the less abundant greenleaf manzanita are common shrubs, along with buckbrush. Redbud, another shrub, displays beautiful reddish-purple flowers in early spring.

Ponderosa Pine Forest (1,200–5,500 feet). The two most characteristic trees, ponderosa pine and Douglas fir, are primary timber trees in California, so you'll often see evidence of logging. Incense cedar, present in large numbers, is the only cedar species native to this part of Northern California. White fir, the only true fir in this plant community, grows in abundance at higher elevations. (Douglas fir is actually a spruce.) The major deciduous trees are black oak, big-leaf maple, and dogwood; all three put on a spectacular visual display in autumn. Greenleaf manzanita and several varieties of ceanothus are common shrubs.

Red Fir Forest (5,500–7,500 feet). As the name indicates, red fir dominates at this elevation range. Jeffrey pine, often mistaken for the similar ponderosa pine, is another common inhabitant. (While both pines share a similar overall appearance and 5- to 10-inch-long needles in bundles of three, Jeffrey pine cones have no sharp points, whereas ponderosa pine cones do. Also, the bark of Jeffrey pine often emits a vanilla odor.) Common shrubs include chinquapin and pine-mat manzanita.

Animals. Since most animals take a siesta during midday, your chances of observing them peak during the early morning and early evening hours. Also, if you're talking on the trail with companions you'll scare away most wildlife: walk quietly with a minimum of conversation. The best way to see the most wildlife is to sit motionless for at least several minutes in an area often frequented by animals, such as a good watering spot.

Mammals. Northern California's two most common large mammals are the mule deer and the black bear. Mule deer thrive from the Central Valley up to the highest elevations, and you should see plenty if you hike often. Bears are both rarer and shyer. When encountered, most will immediately turn tail and skedaddle away at high speed. The only time they present a significant danger is when you get between a mother and her cubs. If this happens, slowly back away. Don't make a sudden run for it; she is faster than you are.

A variety of smaller critters inhabit the Central Valley, foothill woodland, and ponderosa pine forest. You'll often encounter jackrabbits, brushrabbits, chipmunks, gray and ground squirrels, and everyone's perennial favorite, the striped skunk. Raccoons and porcupines present themselves less frequently.

Predators, due to their position at the apex of the food chain, are much fewer in number than the animals listed above. Most common is the coyote, though gray foxes, mountain lions, and bobcats do haunt the wilderness's farther reaches.

Several mammals primarily inhabit aquatic environments. Beaver build dams on streams or make burrows along the banks of the Sacramento River. Otter also frequent the Sacramento River, and seem to have more fun than any other animal on the planet. The nonnative muskrat lives in underwater burrows by still or slow-moving waters.

Birds. Hundreds of different bird species dwell in the region covered by this book. In the Sacramento Valley and surrounding foothills, you'll often see meadowlarks, robins, sparrows, blue jays, bluebirds, blackbirds, crows, and a variety of woodpeckers. Farther up in the ponderosa pine belt live band-tailed pigeons, flickers, and Steller's jays. The red-tailed hawk is the most common predatory bird, but you may also encounter any of several owl species, or even a bald eagle.

Rivers, ponds, and lakes host a variety of birds, some of which reside only part of the year. You can expect to observe Canada and snow geese, mallard and teal ducks, great blue herons, white pelicans, great egrets, and cormorants.

HIKING SAFETY

Some of this book's hikes are flat, short, and close to sources of help if problems should arise. However, many trails travel through wilderness. A host of dangers, such as accidents and adverse weather changes, can cause significant problems for the unprepared.

Traveling alone. If you plan to hike solo, be sure to let a responsible family member or friend know your exact route and the time you expect to arrive home, then call to affirm you are safe and sound. If by chance you are injured or become lost in a remote area, this precaution could save your life.

Clothing. Always put an extra layer of clothing in your daypack. The temperature can drop dramatically, either through a gain in elevation or a change in weather. Include a watchman's cap; it's small and lightweight and will greatly slow heat loss from your head.

A good pair of running or walking shoes serves adequately for most hikes, but lightweight hiking boots provide better ankle support and traction, and are just as comfortable.

Many hikers prefer wearing shorts during the summer months, but read the hike description before you decide. Some hikes can involve cross-country trekking through summer stickers, and poison oak is often present.

A hat keeps the sun off your head and out of your face. Sunglasses protect your eyes.

Food. Snacks provide an energy boost on shorter hikes, and a lunch is a definite must for longer rambles. Avoid foods that are spicy or salty, or that could become a gooey mess in your daypack. Always bring more food than you think you need.

Water. *Giardia,* a microorganism that causes severe intestinal distress, has spread through much of Northern California. Avoid this debilitating (though curable) disease by never drinking untreated water, regardless of how pure it looks. You can treat trailside water using filtration devices available at outdoor supply stores, or through chemical means. Both methods have drawbacks: filters are a hassle; chemicals are a hassle *and* make the water taste terrible. It's best to pack more than enough water from home, and bring one or two small cartons of fruit juice.

Weather. The region covered by this book rarely sees summer rain, though sudden thunderstorms occasionally occur. The other three seasons bring varying amounts of precipitation. Prudence requires minimal preparedness for bad weather. A lightweight poncho can double as a picnic blanket or sitting cushion. Space blankets weigh about 2 ounces and are smaller than a fist. Either can keep you dry and repel the wind, making an unexpected overnight wilderness stay less miserable. And remember that thunderstorms and accompanying lightning can occur any time of year. Whenever the tall thunderheads gather along your route, stay among the shorter trees of the forest, far away from exposed ridges and promontories.

Hypothermia. This debilitating and sometimes fatal physical condition, marked by a drastic drop in body temperature, is caused by a combination of cold, wind, wetness, and fatigue. Symptoms include shivering, loss of coordination, and inarticulate speech. Avoid hypothermia by wearing warm clothes (including a windbreaker or parka), staying dry, and choosing hikes well within the limits of your physical ability. If you (or a hiking companion) develop hypothermia symptoms, find shelter from any wind or rain, replace wet clothing with dry clothing if possible, and build a fire for warmth. Also, eat foods with lots of sugar and starch, such as breads and candy. The body quickly converts these carbohydrates to energy and ultimately heat.

Recommended supplies. For all wilderness hikes you'll want to bring a first aid kit, knife, matches, fire starter (for use with wet wood), flashlight, sunscreen, and toilet paper. Good topographical maps and a compass will help you navigate if you should become lost.

Rattlesnakes. These poisonous reptiles present a real danger, though hikers will seldom encounter them. Mostly active during the warmer months, they frequent rocky places, brush, and occasionally the sides of trails. Distinguished by a jointed rattle at the end of the tail, they usually strike only when cornered or touched. Minimize chance meetings by watching the trail ahead and being especially alert when hiking cross-country.

Ticks. With the spread of the tick-borne Lyme disease, these little bugs have become more than a minor nuisance. They frequent bushes and tall grasses, hoping to brush against an animal so they can subsequently attach themselves and dine on their host's blood. Pants and long sleeves help prevent problems with ticks, as does a thorough check of scalp and skin at the

Poison oak leaves; note the three leaf clusters.

end of the hike. If one does attach itself, attempt a careful and complete removal with tweezers, or use a tick removal kit. If this doesn't work, or if
you suffer any adverse reaction after a tick bite, visit a doctor.

Poison oak. This pesky shrub can grow at elevations as high as 5,000 feet,
and sports beautiful red foliage in autumn. Although it takes a variety of
disguises, from a climbing vine to a dense hillside thicket, its one constant
characteristic is a cluster of three leaves. The leaves themselves can vary in
shape and size, so always assume a three-leafed plant is the real McCoy.
Poison oak can cause an irritating, painful skin rash. Wash exposed areas
thoroughly with soap and water. Also, follow my mother's advice: Don't
scratch! Commercially available creams help ameliorate the symptoms.

Hiking ethics. Preservation philosophy should be your inner guide when
hiking. Leave the wilderness as unspoiled as the way you found it: no trace
of your visit should remain.

Your feet can do a lot of damage. Always stay on the main trail: short-cutting across switchbacks quickly leads to erosion. And when hiking cross-country, don't trample delicate plants or disturb the ground. Walk on rock or firm soil whenever possible.

A NOTE ABOUT SAFETY

Safety is an important concern in all outdoor activities. No guidebook can alert you to every hazard or anticipate the limitations of every reader. Therefore, the descriptions of roads, trails, routes, and natural features in this book are not representations that a particular place or excursion will be safe for your party. When you follow any of the routes described in this book, you assume responsibility for your own safety. Under normal conditions, such excursions require the usual attention to traffic, road and trail conditions, weather, terrain, the capabilities of your party, and other factors. Keeping informed on current conditions and exercising common sense are the keys to a safe, enjoyable outing.

The Mountaineers

HOW TO USE THIS BOOK

At the beginning of each hike description you'll find in summary form all the pertinent information necessary to gain a basic feel for the hike. The main body of the text covers how to get to the trailhead, specific details of the hike's highlights, a discussion of various aspects of trailside natural and human history, and enough directional guidance to ensure that you won't get lost.

Here's how to make the best use of the information at the beginning of each hike description:

Jurisdiction and information. Gives the address and phone number of the agency responsible for the specific trail. These agencies can provide you with current trail information and weather conditions. They often have a wide variety of brochures, and usually stock maps that show the hiking trails.

Length. Represents the one-way distance, unless noted otherwise, and was determined from maps, official measurements, and/or estimates based on pace and the time to complete the hike.

Difficulty. This subjective indicator takes into account both the fatigue factor of longer trails and the amount of agility and ability you'll need to get safely through any dangerous areas along the way. An "Easy" rating indicates that the trail is mostly flat, has few if any dangerous spots, and is suited for hikers of all ages and abilities. A "Moderate" rating indicates a hike for the more experienced, and can involve sections of steep, slippery trail, a lot of elevation gain, and/or a long distance to cover. A "Strenuous" rating indicates that only those in good shape and possessing considerable hiking experience, including familiarity with cross-country hiking, should attempt the route.

Starting point. Gives the trailhead's elevation.

High (or low) point. Gives the highest (or lowest) elevation attained during the hike. By comparing this value with the starting point elevation you can get a good idea of the total elevation change of the hike.

Trail characteristics. Indicates the nature of the trail's surface, and whether certain trail sections are unusually steep or slippery.

Uses. Hiking is allowed on all trails. However, mountainbikes and horses are allowed only on some trails. Appendices 1 and 2 at the end of the book specifically list trails for mountainbikes and horses. Be aware of the increasing trend towards restricting these two forms of wilderness transportation. Call the information number to clarify current policy. Appendix 3 lists trails suitable for young children.

Season. You can hike almost all trails in this book throughout the year. Only a few at higher elevations receive enough snow to block access in winter and spring. However, many of the hikes are at an elevation of 1,500 to 3,000 feet and can receive temporary snow cover. If you are unsure about a trail's current status, call the relevant information number.

Hiking a trail in different seasons offers the opportunity to observe the complete turn of nature's cycle. In spring, flowers bloom, deciduous trees burst forth in verdant hues, and temperatures are mild. In summer, many flowers continue to show color, and the fully leaved trees shelter you from the sun's warm rays. Autumn ushers in bright, radiant colors that play against the greens of pines, firs, and cedars. Winter offers more solitude on the trails, and surprises you with the unexpected activity of birds and mammals.

Facilities. Lists toilets, showers, and recreational facilities near the trailhead.

Water. Gives all sources of potentially drinkable water, including drinking fountains and year-round and seasonal creeks. Remember to purify any water not brought from home or obtained from a fountain or faucet.

Regarding driving directions. These lead you from the nearest major town or highway to the trailhead. All roads to the trailheads are paved or maintained dirt and gravel (unless noted otherwise) and should not prove difficult for any vehicle to navigate. Odometers (mileage meters) vary in accuracy, so look for intersections, turnoffs, etc. before you've traveled the specified distance.

Regarding hunting seasons. Legal hunting seasons run from early September through late January. Since peace, quiet, and the opportunity to observe wildlife are primary goals for most hikers, you may want to avoid certain areas during hunting seasons. For specific information on exact hunting season dates, and whether or not hunting is allowed in the area you plan to hike, contact the California Fish and Game Department, 601 Locust Street, Redding, CA 96001, (916) 225-2300. Wear brightly colored clothes if you decide to hike during hunting season.

Regarding maps. Trail maps are provided for most hikes in this book but are intended for reference only. A few of the shorter trails near towns have a mapboard at the trailhead, or a brochure with map; these maps are not duplicated here. Hikers should get USGS or Forest Service maps for navigation purposes.

The following symbols are used in all this book's maps:

MAP LEGEND

=====	INTERSTATE HIGHWAYS	⬯	INTERSTATE HIGHWAY
———	PAVED ROADS	⬯	U.S. HIGHWAY
— — —	GRAVEL OR DIRT ROADS	◯	STATE HIGHWAY
～～～	TRAIL	◯	COUNTY ROAD
··········	CROSS COUNTRY - FAINT TRAIL	Ⓟ	PARKING AREA
▱	WATER BODY	△	CAMPGROUND
～···～	INTERMITTENT STREAM	▲	MOUNTAIN PEAK
～～	RIVER	■	SITE, POINT OF INTEREST
～～	WATERFALL	⇥⟞ BRIDGE ⊢ GATE	
～～	BOUNDARY	⤬	PICNIC AREA
○	CITY OR TOWN	†	CEMETERY

CHAPTER ONE
. . . .
Castle Crags State Park and Vicinity

The jagged granite spires and slabs of Castle Crags would appear more at home in the Swiss Alps, and contrast sharply with both the surrounding forested mountains and the volcanic Cascade Range to the north and east.

Of the trails in the area, only the Castle Dome Trail (hike 6), the most strenuous in the chapter, actually goes into the Crags. The other trails within the park travel at lower elevations through thick forests, though some allow occasional glimpses of the Crags. Of special interest are the Indian Creek Trail (hike 1), an interpretive nature hike which allows you to learn about local human and natural history, and the River Trail (hike 8), which runs upstream along the Sacramento River. Outside the park, the Pacific Crest Trail (PCT, hike 9) and the Burstarse Falls Trail (hike 10), are both moderately strenuous hikes that have numerous open views of the Crags and surrounding mountains. In addition, the Burstarse Falls Trail takes you to the foot of Burstarse Falls, an impressive 40-foot cascade during spring and early summer. The Twin Lakes/ Tamarack Lake Trail (hike 11), the westernmost hike in this chapter, takes you 6,000 feet up into the mixed fir forest, and allows you to visit three lakes and climb a mountain that boasts a panoramic 360-degree view.

Besides hiking, the area offers other recreational opportunities. Anglers will want to try their luck at the Sacramento River, and the steep spires of the Crags will challenge even expert rock climbers. (Don't attempt such climbs unless you are an *experienced* rock climber.)

Castle Crags are the remnants of molten rock forced towards the earth's surface about 170 million years ago by the heat generated from the floor of the Pacific Ocean sliding under California. The magnificently shaped granite we see today is the result of a combination of millions of years of wind and water erosion, which carried soft rock and soil away, and glacial action, which carved and polished the granite. The Crags lie on the eastern edge of the Klamath Mountains, which were split long ago from the Sierra Nevada mountains and pushed northwest.

A wide variety of plant life flourishes in and around the park. At lower elevations ponderosa pines and live and black oaks predominate, whereas

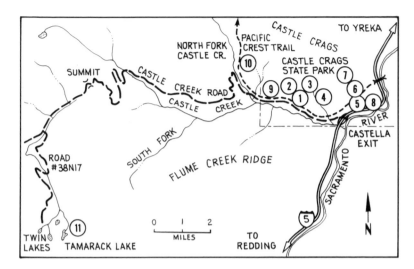

up near the base of the Crags, red fir trees grow in abundance. Wildflowers, dispersed throughout the park, peak in late spring and early summer.

Overnight campers could gain firsthand knowledge regarding the presence of bears. An alert observer may also see deer, squirrels, raccoons, coyotes, gray foxes, and, in the upper reaches of the Crags, mountain lions. In addition, many species of birds live in the park.

Native Americans first inhabited this region, but inevitably came into conflict with "civilized" man's insatiable desire for land and wealth. The whites' unsuccessful search for gold in the region during the early 1850s silted up local streams and the Sacramento River, thereby destroying the fish that provided a mainstay of the natives' diet. This led to clashes and, ultimately, deaths on both sides.

The coming of the Southern Pacific Railroad along the Sacramento River in the 1880s opened the way for extensive mining and timber operations, and evidence of these activities is found throughout the park. You'll see old water pipes and flumes, and areas that look as if they were logged many years ago. The park headquarters sit on the site of an old chromium mine, and the Indian Creek Nature Trail briefly passes over some of the mine's resultant tailings.

Hotels in the nearby town of Castella served travelers making their way through the mountains by train or wagon. Also, many area resorts thrived on the reputation of the purported healing powers of mineral water from local springs. Around the turn of the century this water was bottled and marketed as the famous "Castle Rock Natural Mineral Water."

Castle Crags State Park campground has 64 campsites (reservations necessary May 1 to September 30) and several buildings which contain both toilets and hot showers. Fees are charged for camping and park entrance.

. . . .

1 INDIAN CREEK TRAIL

Jurisdiction and information: Castle Crags State Park, P.O. Box 80, Castella, CA 96017. (916) 235-2684.
Length: 1.0-mile loop
Difficulty: Easy
Starting point: 2,060 feet
High point: 2,220 feet
Trail characteristics: Flat dirt path
Uses: Hiking
Season: Year-round
Facilities: Toilets and showers in park campground
Water: Available at park headquarters and from Indian Creek
Map: USGS Dunsmuir

The Indian Creek Nature Trail offers a good way to acquaint yourself with the rich human and natural history of the Castle Crags area. An excellent brochure prepared by the Castle Crags Interpretive Association (available

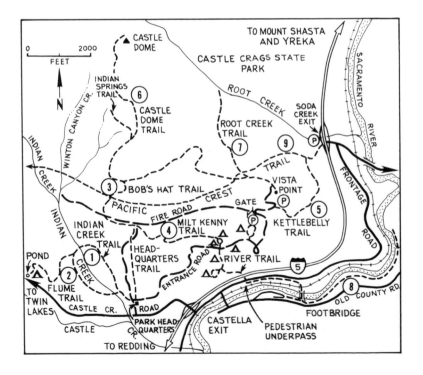

from park headquarters for a small fee) gives detailed explanations of what you'll see at the twenty-nine numbered posts located along the trail.

Evidence of man's exploitation of local natural resources abounds. You'll see old flumes and ditches that once transported water, the remains of engine-drawn cable systems once used to remove timber, and chromium ore tailings (now replanted with ponderosa pine). But don't despair too much at the disruptive activities of humans: you'll learn to identify twenty-one different trees and shrubs, and gain knowledge of the process by which rock slowly turns to soil through the combined efforts of plants, animals, and microscopic organisms. Beautiful views of Castle Crags towering high above and the soothing presence of clear, cool Indian Creek provide the finishing touches for a hike that suits all, young and old.

Take the Castle Crags State Park/Castella exit off I-5, which is 48 miles north of Redding and 6 miles south of Dunsmuir. Follow the signs and head west. After 0.25 mile turn right, and park by park headquarters.

One hundred yards from the trailhead you'll come to a fork. It's best to go left, because the numbered posts run clockwise. The trail climbs very gently over the first 0.5 mile, then just as gently descends back to its starting point. One hundred yards past post 16 the Flume Trail comes in on the left. This trail, described in a separate entry, makes a nice addition to your hike.

· ·

2 FLUME TRAIL

Jurisdiction and information: Castle Crags State Park, P.O. Box 80, Castella, CA 96017. (916) 235-2684.
Length: 0.75 mile one way
Difficulty: Easy
Starting point: 2,100 feet
High point: 2,200 feet
Trail characteristics: Mostly flat, easy walking on a dirt path
Uses: Hiking
Season: Year-round
Facilities: Toilets and showers in park campground, outhouse near the trail's end at Castle Creek Road
Water: Available at park headquarters and from small seasonal streams
Map: USGS Dunsmuir

This trail will most likely be used by those also hiking the Indian Creek Trail (hike 1). Well shaded along its entire length, it travels through dense stands of Douglas fir and ponderosa pine.

Leaves and needles partially fill the old wooden flume along the Flume Trail.

It can be accessed from both ends, but is described here as beginning from the Indian Creek Trail (hike 1). Proceed 0.5 mile up the Indian Creek Trail (be sure to bear left at the fork) to where the signed Flume Creek Trail comes in on the left. To reach the other access point, go 1.0 mile down Castle Creek Road from the west side of the Castle Crags State Park/ Castella exit off I-5. There's no sign, but along the right-hand side of the road you'll see a low rock wall and two garbage cans on a post. Walk past the dammed pond towards the environmental campsites to the signed trail.

From where it starts at the Indian Creek Trail, the Flume Trail almost immediately begins to parallel closely the elevated wooden flume from which it gets its name. The flume is part of an old system that brought water from Castle Creek to Castella. You're welcome to inspect the flume and other human artifacts you may find, but please don't disturb them.

About 0.5 mile from the trail's beginning you'll cross a wooden bridge over a small creek. The path then travels alongside an old ditch that was part of the same water delivery system as the flume, finally descending a few hundred yards later to the environmental campsites by Castle Creek Road. Be sure to check out the pond, which hosts a variety of aquatic plant species and associated animal life.

· ·

3 HEADQUARTERS TRAIL/BOB'S HAT TRAIL

Jurisdiction and information: Castle Crags State Park, P.O. Box 80, Castella, CA 96017. (916) 235-2684.
Length: 1.6 miles one way to the Castle Dome Trail
Difficulty: Moderate
Starting point: 2,060 feet
High point: 3,300 feet
Trail characteristics: Ranges from good dirt trail to wide dirt road
Uses: Hiking
Season: Year-round
Facilities: Toilets and showers in campground
Water: Available in campground and at park headquarters
Map: USGS Dunsmuir

This combination of trails and dirt roads provides an alternate route up to the Crags as it passes through thick forests of towering ponderosa pine and Douglas fir on its way up to the Castle Dome Trail. You'll get a good workout from the over 1,200-foot elevation gain—the trail starts climbing almost immediately and never flattens out. It's well shaded in some areas, but much of it follows exposed dirt roads. Be sure to bring water.

Take the Castle Crags State Park/Castella exit off I-5, which is 48 miles north of Redding and 6 miles south of Dunsmuir. Follow the signs and head west. After 0.25 mile turn right, where you'll find park headquarters. The trail begins on the left about 200 feet up the main road from park headquarters. It's marked with a "trail" sign.

The route initially travels through a dense forest of ponderosa pines. After a few hundred yards it joins a dirt road, which you follow uphill. (If you are ever in doubt as to which way to go when trying to navigate this maze of roads and trails, just take the steepest route uphill. Luckily, all trail forks are signed.) Two hundred yards up this road the Milt Kenny Trail (hike 4)

A towering stand of ponderosa pine provides deep shade at the beginning of the Headquarters Trail/Bob's Hat Trail.

comes in from the right, and 100 yards farther is another dirt road. As a sign will indicate, go left. After 0.5 mile you must turn right on another fire road. Three-quarters of a mile uphill from this fork you'll hit the Pacific Crest Trail (hike 9). Go left on this famous path for a whole 100 feet, then turn right at a trail fork. One-quarter mile farther is the Castle Dome Trail (hike 6). Reaching the Dome entails another 1.9 miles of uphill hiking.

Keep in mind that there are several combinations of trails that can be taken in conjunction with the Headquarters Trail/Bob's Hat Trail. The map will help you plan your itinerary.

4 MILT KENNY TRAIL

Jurisdiction and information: Castle Crags State Park, P.O. Box 80, Castella, CA 96017. (916) 235-2684.
Length: 0.9 mile one way
Difficulty: Easy
Starting point: 2,100 feet
High point: 2,200 feet
Trail characteristics: Wide, flat trail provides easy walking
Uses: Hiking
Season: Year-round
Facilities: Toilets and showers in campground
Water: Available in campground
Map: USGS Dunsmuir

This nearly flat trail provides a nice stroll under the shade of ponderosa pines, Douglas firs, and black oaks. Families with small children will appreciate its easy hiking, and those staying in the campground will enjoy its accessibility.

Take the Castle Crags State Park/Castella exit off I-5, which is 48 miles north of Redding and 6 miles south of Dunsmuir. Follow the signs and head west. After 0.25 mile turn right, where you'll find park headquarters. From park headquarters turn right and follow the paved road 0.7 mile to a crossroad in the campground. Go left and park.

To begin the hike, go through the Pacific Crest Trail campsite, where a sign will get you started. Parts of the path run along the old Root Creek logging railroad line, though the tracks themselves have long since been removed. Look for the remains of foundations that once supported the train's watering tanks.

The trail ends at the Headquarters Trail/Bob's Hat Trail, and could be used as a way to connect with many of the other trails in the park, such as the Castle Dome Trail (hike 6) and PCT (hike 9).

5 KETTLEBELLY TRAIL

Jurisdiction and information: Castle Crags State Park, P.O. Box 80, Castella, CA 96017. (916) 235-2684.
Length: 1.0 mile one way
Difficulty: Easy to moderate
Starting point: 2,300 feet
Low point: 2,100 feet
Trail characteristics: Trail, though covered with leaves and pine needles, is generally easy walking
Uses: Hiking
Season: Year-round
Facilities: Toilets and showers in campground
Water: Available in campground only
Map: USGS Dunsmuir

The Kettlebelly Trail provides a pleasant walk on a little-used path through thick groves of ponderosa pine, and serves as a shortcut to the campground for Pacific Crest Trail hikers. It also passes through an area rich in railroad history. Part of the path follows the railroad line, built by the Castle Crags Lumber Company in 1922, which crossed Kettlebelly Ridge over to Root Creek.

Take the Castle Crags State Park/Castella exit off I-5, which is 48 miles north of Redding and 6 miles south of Dunsmuir. Follow the signs and head west. After 0.25 mile turn right, where you'll find park headquarters.

From park headquarters turn right and follow the paved road through the campground towards the vista point and Castle Dome trailhead. After about 1.0 mile you'll see a dirt road on the left. Park here, but be careful not to block the fire road gate. Then walk 100 feet up the road to the signed Kettlebelly Trail.

To begin, go around the locked green gate at the trailhead. The trail, thick with pine needles, gently descends over a 1.0-mile course to its end at the PCT. Once there you can either hike up towards the other trails and sights in Castle Crags State Park, go down 0.4 mile to the PCT access point by the Soda Creek exit off I-5, or return the way you came.

It's also possible to make a round-trip loop by walking the Kettlebelly

Black oak leaves

Trail (hike 5), the PCT (hike 9), the Headquarters Trail/Bob's Hat Trail (hike 3), and the dirt road that meets the Vista Point Road at the Kettlebelly Trail parking area (see map).

6 CASTLE DOME TRAIL

Jurisdiction and information: Castle Crags State Park, P.O. Box 80, Castella, CA 96017. (916) 235-2684.
Length: 2.9 miles one way
Difficulty: Strenuous
Starting point: 2,600 feet
High point: 4,700 feet
Trail characteristics: Good surface to the junction of Indian Springs Trail; rocky and occasionally slippery afterwards
Uses: Hiking
Season: Year-round
Facilities: Toilets and showers in campground, pit toilet at trailhead parking lot
Water: Available only at Indian Springs, which is 2.0 miles up the trail
Map: USGS Dunsmuir

This hike provides the most spectacular scenery found in the park, but you will have to pay a price—namely, climbing 2,100 feet in less than 3 miles. Still, when you see Mount Shasta holding court in regal splendor to the north, the sheer granite faces of the Crags piercing the sky to the west, and the rest of far Northern California spread out before you, you'll surely agree that the exertion was worthwhile.

Take the Castle Crags State Park/Castella exit off I-5, which is 48 miles north of Redding and 6 miles south of Dunsmuir. Follow the signs and head west. After 0.25 mile turn right, where you'll find park headquarters.

From park headquarters, turn right and drive up the paved road through the campground. Signs for photography and the vista point help guide you, but pay close attention or you'll get an unwanted tour of all the campsites. The road becomes very narrow and curvy as it climbs the last mile to the trailhead, and this last stretch is very difficult for recreational vehicles and cars with trailers. You can also reach the Castle Dome Trail from both the Pacific Crest Trail (hike 9) and Headquarters Trail/Bob's Hat Trail (hike 3).

To begin the hike, follow the road back 150 feet from the parking area to where the signed trail begins on the right. The first 0.25 mile of trail stays flat, but after a left turn at the junction with the Root Creek Trail (hike 7) it's an uphill push all the way. After a few minutes of climbing you'll cross the famous PCT (hike 9). About 1.0 mile from the trailhead lies yet another intersection, this time with the Bob's Hat Trail (hike 3).

A mile farther, the short Indian Springs Trail takes off on the left. Indian Springs offers the only source of water for Castle Dome–bound hikers. The easy, flat, 0.25-mile walk provides excellent views of the Flume Creek Ridge just south of the park. The water at Indian Springs seeps out of cracks in the rock face, and the area is lush, cool, and well shaded by big-leaf maple, dogwood, and incense cedar trees.

As you continue up the Castle Dome Trail, the Douglas fir, ponderosa pine, live oak, and black oak that grow at lower elevations fall behind. You'll now encounter true firs around the area where the trail becomes much more rocky. The first tantalizing views of the Crags and Mount Shasta appear as the trail climbs up to the base of the Crags, and eventually to the base of Castle Dome itself.

Now that you have reached the end of the trail, enjoy the spectacular scenery. For the best views of Mount Shasta, walk to the saddle near the dome, where a chain fence keeps you from falling. To the south you'll see the Grey Rocks of Flume Ridge, just on the other side of the Castle Creek Valley. Shasta Bally and Bully Choop lie farther south, and to the east are Girard Ridge and the forested mountains on the other side of the Sacramento River. A look down into the valley shows the river far below, with the town of Dunsmuir to the northeast.

Some people climb to the top of Castle Dome. The route followed by most begins on the south side of the dome, then follows a crack around towards the east side. Be aware that it's very easy to slip and fall when climbing on steep rock, and even a short fall could result in serious injury or death. Do not attempt the climb if you have shoes with poor tread, if the rock is wet, or if you are unsure of the route.

To return to the trailhead you must go back the way you came. If you still have energy, the Indian Springs Trail and the Root Creek Trail (hike 7) offer good side trips. Don't forget to see the breathtaking views of Mount Shasta and the Crags from the vista point above the trailhead parking lot.

. . . .

7 ROOT CREEK TRAIL

Jurisdiction and information: Castle Crags State Park, P.O. Box 80, Castella, CA 96017. (916) 235-2684.
Length: 1.0 mile one way
Difficulty: Easy
Starting point: 2,600 feet
High point: 2,750 feet
Trail characteristics: Flat dirt trail
Uses: Hiking
Season: Year-round
Facilities: Toilets and showers in campground, pit toilet at trailhead parking lot
Water: Available from Root Creek
Map: USGS Dunsmuir

The Root Creek Trail provides a pleasant walk along a flat path that's well shaded by Douglas firs and ponderosa pines. It's a great hike for families with small children, or anyone who wants nice scenery and quietude without much effort.

Take the Castle Crags State Park/Castella exit off I-5, which is 48 miles north of Redding and 6 miles south of Dunsmuir. Follow the signs and head west. After 0.25 mile turn right, where you'll find park headquarters. From here, follow the hike 6 directions to the trailhead.

The trail begins 150 feet down the road from the parking area. After 0.25 mile the Castle Dome Trail (hike 6) heads upwards to the foot of the Crags. Stay to the right. A few hundred feet later the path briefly joins the Pacific Crest Trail (hike 9) for 200 yards, then forks left to Root Creek.

At the trail's end you can sit on one of the benches situated by the creek and relax in the shade of alders, vine maples, and cedars. The creek itself gurgles contentedly as it cascades over boulders in a series of 3-foot waterfalls. This spot is quite isolated: you won't hear any freeway noise and most people tend to hike the Castle Dome Trail, leaving Root Creek for the knowing few. To the west, the Crags peek through the trees, though you'll have to look hard to see them. Some of Root Creek's pools are large enough to wade in, with the largest pool located about 100 yards downstream from the trail's end.

The River Trail's footbridge allows safe passage across the upper Sacramento River's rushing waters.

8 RIVER TRAIL

Jurisdiction and information: Castle Crags State Park, P.O. Box 80, Castella, CA 96017. (916) 235-2684.
Length: 1.4 miles one way
Difficulty: Easy to moderate
Starting point: 2,050 feet
High point: 2,100 feet
Trail characteristics: Relatively flat dirt path, but slippery in places
Uses: Hiking
Season: Year-round
Facilities: Toilets and showers at the campground and a nearby picnic area, which require entrance fees
Water: Available from a trailside drinking fountain located 50 feet east of the railroad tracks
Map: USGS Dunsmuir

The River Trail is the only trail in the area that goes along the Sacramento River. The river makes its way from the slopes of northern mountains through the upper canyon area (where this trail is located) to Shasta Lake and finally through the Delta to San Francisco Bay and the Pacific Ocean.

From the Castle Crags State Park/Castella exit off I-5 go east and turn left onto Frontage Road. One-half mile down this road is a wide shoulder on the right, which fronts several picnic sites. Drive to the end of this wide shoulder, where a "River Trail" sign marks the trailhead. (The trailhead can also be reached from the eastern edge of the park campground. A trail goes under the freeway and then follows the frontage road.)

From the trailhead, follow the trail down some steps and under the railroad tracks. (A drinking fountain is located on the right just past the tracks.) After crossing the river by footbridge, turn left and follow the trail northward. For the next 0.5 mile the trail undulates gently about 50 feet above the river's banks, providing the only views of Castle Crags. Several faint, steep trails give access to the river. The last 0.75 mile of trail runs flatter and much closer to the river, and is very popular with fishermen and rafters. You'll cross Fall Creek 1.0 mile from the footbridge, and less than 0.5 mile farther come to the end of the trail.

Notice the variety of vegetation all along the trail. Near the river, riparian trees such as willows and alders use the stream to meet their requirements for large amounts of water. Farther away are Douglas firs, ponderosa pines, and big-leaf maples, which can live on less water and are found at lower elevations throughout Castle Crags State Park and the mountains of Northern California.

9 PACIFIC CREST TRAIL

Jurisdiction and information: Mount Shasta Ranger District, Shasta National Forest, 204 West Alma, Mount Shasta, CA 96067. (916) 926-4511.
Length: 6.7 miles one way to the Dog Trail intersection
Difficulty: Moderate to strenuous
Starting point: 2,000 feet
High point: 2,950 feet
Trail characteristics: Generally good footing, although there are areas of loose rock and dirt
Uses: Hiking, horseback riding
Season: Year-round
Facilities: None
Water: Available year-round from several creeks
Map: USGS Dunsmuir

The Pacific Crest Trail (PCT) stretches from Mexico to Canada, and encompasses some of the most beautiful scenery in the western United States. This entry describes the portion of the PCT that passes through Castle Crags State Park and adjoining portions of the Shasta National Forest. Scenery ranges from shaded forest to shaded mountain streams to breathtaking vistas of Castle Crags to rather mundane stretches of trail that are hot and exposed. This hike is described as beginning from the Soda Creek exit off I-5, but the PCT can be better accessed from the Castle Dome Trail (hike 6), Root Creek Trail (hike 7), Headquarters Trail/Bob's Hat Trail (hike 3), and Burstarse Falls/Dog Trail (hike 10), with the Castle Dome Trail being your best bet. You can make your own decision as to which portions of the PCT you wish to hike. You may want to consider hiking to the Dog Trail and having somebody pick you up there. (For directions see the Burstarse Falls entry [hike 10].)

The PCT is easy to follow: all trail intersections are signed, and you'll soon learn to recognize the triangular PCT symbol posted at irregular intervals along the route. Watch out for occasional poison oak.

Take the Soda Creek exit off I-5, which is 1.0 mile north of the Castella/Castle Crags exit. The trail starts 100 feet west of the freeway, by a locked green gate.

To begin the hike, go around the locked green gate and follow the paved road that leads to the left. This road quickly turns to dirt trail and heads up-hill. The Kettlebelly Trail (hike 5) enters from the left 0.4 mile from the trailhead. Go right. About 1.0 mile farther you intersect the Root Creek Trail (hike 7), 0.2 mile farther the Castle Dome Trail (hike 6), and another 0.5 mile farther the Headquarters Trail/Bob's Hat Trail (hike 3). After you encounter the last of these signed trail intersections it's smooth sailing for the rest of the hike.

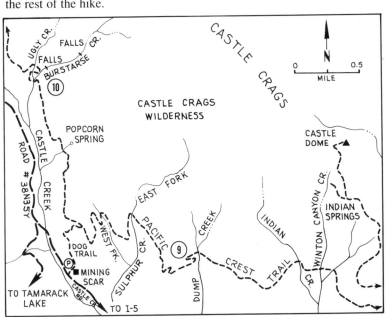

A few hundred yards past this last trail intersection are the first views of the Crags and surrounding mountains. You then arrive at the creek that flows from Indian Springs high above, which also serves as the source of Castle Crags State Park's drinking water. Just past this creek flows well-shaded Winton Canyon Creek, with its accompanying alders, ferns, and tiger lilies. And when it rains it pours, for just past Winton Canyon Creek is Indian Creek, another year-round stream that sports pools deep enough to submerge your sweaty body if you're hiking in summer.

The trail then leaves the ponderosa pines, Douglas firs, and various oaks behind as it undulates through exposed areas that allow exquisite views of the Crags. One and a half miles past Indian Creek runs the oddly named Dump Creek. You then climb a ridge covered with knobcone pines. These trees are easily identified by the cones tightly bound to the trunks. Knobcone pines only release seeds after a fire, so as long as forest fires are controlled the knobcone will have great difficulty perpetuating itself.

About 0.6 mile past the knobcone pine grove the trail encounters the east fork of Sulphur Creek, a shaded year-round stream. One-half mile farther the even prettier west fork of Sulphur Creek serves as a great place to eat lunch and soak your feet. The trail then heads uphill, offering the most spectacular views of the Crags so far, then intersects the Dog Trail 0.6 mile from the west fork of Sulphur Creek. If you wish, you can hike another 2.0 miles along the PCT to Burstarse Falls (hike 10).

. . . .

10 BURSTARSE FALLS

Jurisdiction and information: Mount Shasta Ranger District, 204 West Alma, Mount Shasta, CA 96067. (916) 926-4511.
Length: 2.6 miles one way
Difficulty: Moderate
Starting point: 2,450 feet
High point: 3,250 feet
Trail characteristics: First 0.5 mile is steep, rocky, and exposed; remainder is shaded and climbs gently
Uses: Hiking, horseback riding
Season: Year-round
Facilities: None
Water: Available year-round from Popcorn Spring, Ugly Creek, and Burstarse Creek
Map: USGS Dunsmuir

In addition to the beauty and solitude of Burstarse Falls, this hike offers open views of Castle Crags and the surrounding mountains. Note that it involves some steep slope scrambling and rock hopping to actually get to the falls. Also, much of the hike passes through an environmentally sensitive area, so please stay on the trail.

From the Castella/Castle Crags State Park exit off I-5 go to the west side of the freeway and get on Castle Creek Road. Follow this road about 3.2 miles to where you see a large scar from mining operations in the hillside on the right. Turn in and park.

To begin, go to the west side of the parking area (the left side as you drove in) where you'll see the unmarked Dog Trail heading uphill. The rocky path climbs steeply for most of its 0.6 mile length. But take heart: once you hit the Pacific Crest Trail (PCT) (hike 9) you'll have relatively smooth sailing to Burstarse Falls, with only a few gentle swells to surmount.

When you reach the junction point of the two trails, turn left. (If you turn right you'll reach Sulphur Creek after an easy 0.5 mile walk, and enjoy fantastic views of the Crags in the bargain. Sulphur Creek itself warrants a visit, even if Burstarse Falls isn't on your itinerary.) For the rest of the hike, Douglas firs, ponderosa pines, incense cedars, and black oaks provide ample shade.

After traveling 1.0 mile along the PCT you'll reach Popcorn Spring. Water glides serenely over smooth granite slabs under the shade of maples and oaks, but nothing about this pretty yet ordinary water flow suggests popcorn.

Six-tenths of a mile past Popcorn Spring you'll have your first encounter with Burstarse Creek. Don't get your hopes up, you aren't near the falls yet. Continue up the trail, where views of the Crags and a glimpse of the falls will spur you on to your destination.

A bit less than 0.5 mile from the crossing of Burstarse Creek you'll reach the inappropriately named Ugly Creek. Granted, brushy manzanita and small live oaks border its banks here, but its waters are clear and cool and no doubt pass through prettier scenery downstream.

Two hundred yards past Ugly Creek the trail makes an abrupt 180-degree switchback. Burstarse Creek is 50 feet east of the trail, and the falls await you 100 yards upstream.

To get to the falls, you must first get down to the creek. Accomplish this by carefully making your way down the steep, crumbling granite, being careful not to slip or brush against poison oak.

Once at the creek, go upstream along the far side, where a faint trail will guide you through the rocks. Take note of a small wading pool in the creek that offers a chance to cool off on hot days.

After a couple of minutes of cross-country scrambling at the foot of a sheer rock wall you'll finally attain the main goal of this hike: Burstarse Falls. The falls boasts an unimpeded 40-foot drop, and makes the strongest impression during spring months when water flow is greatest. However, even in other seasons the beautiful canyon and rock walls are well worth the visit, and you'll always enjoy the shade and seclusion.

If you desire more hiking, continue another 0.5 mile on the Pacific Crest Trail in the direction you've been heading to North Branch Creek. Or, on the way back to the trailhead, continue past the Dog Trail turnoff to the cool, shaded waters of Sulphur Creek.

11   TWIN LAKES/TAMARACK LAKE TRAIL

Jurisdiction and information: Mount Shasta Ranger District, 204 West Alma, Mount Shasta, CA 96067. (916) 926-4511.
Length: 1.0 mile one way to Tamarack Lake
Difficulty: Easy to moderate
Starting point: 5,800 feet
High point: 5,950 feet
Trail characteristics: Easy walking to Upper Twin Lake, then rocky and brushy to Tamarack Lake
Uses: Hiking, horseback riding
Season: June to September
Facilities: Primitive campsites at the trailhead
Water: Available from streams and lakes
Map: USGS Dunsmuir

A cross-country hike along a ridge offers unobstructed views of Tamarack Lake.

The combination of three pretty lakes, great views, and easy access makes this hike one of the book's best. It's a good place to bring the whole family because everyone can find something fun to do. The more adventurous can take a cross-country hike up to the ridge above the lakes. Others can relax at the lakes themselves, swimming and fishing to their hearts' content. This hike also makes an excellent summer trip: the high elevation means relatively cool temperatures compared with the low-lying Sacramento Valley.

Take Castle Creek Road (also known as Whalan Road and Road 25) from the west side of the Castella/Castle Crags State Park exit off I-5. The road surface changes from good pavement to passable dirt and gravel. After a few miles the road climbs in earnest, giving nice views of Castle Crags and Flume Creek Ridge. Eleven miles from I-5 you'll reach the road's highest point, which is also the divide between the Trinity and Sacramento river drainages. Nine-tenths mile past the summit the road forks—stay left on Road 25. One-half mile farther the road forks once again. This time you leave Road 25, going left on Road 38N17. Follow this road for 3.0 miles, where you'll come to another fork in the road. (Going left for 100 feet would bring you to a creek crossing. This is not the right way.) You must take the right fork and follow the extremely bumpy road 1.0 mile up to the trailhead. Some vehicles will have difficulty over this last stretch. You may need to park near the last fork and walk to the trailhead.

The signed trail begins at the edge of a beautiful meadow that sports green grasses and a profusion of wildflowers in spring and summer. This meadow was once a lake that slowly filled with sediment, a fate that eventually befalls virtually every lake.

The trail goes along the west side of the meadow for 200 yards, climbs gently through fir trees and crosses a small creek. Less than 0.5 mile from the trailhead you'll come to shallow Lower Twin Lake, which is almost entirely surrounded by forest. Hiking 400 yards farther brings you to the larger, prettier, and much deeper Upper Twin Lake. This lake offers the most recreational opportunities, and since few people come here, you

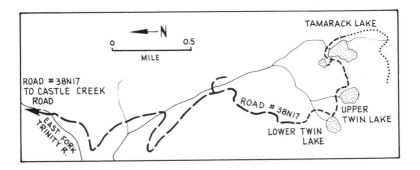

should have it all to yourself. There are good views of the rocky ridge to the south, and the lake reflects the surrounding forest of white firs, Jeffrey pines, and incense cedars. The water, quite warm in summertime, deepens quickly once you swim a few feet from shore. A trail runs along the east (left) side of the lake, giving access to good picnicking and swimming sites. This is an excellent place to camp if you're willing to pack in supplies. (There are also several campsites at the trailhead.)

The main trail becomes rocky and brushy as it goes east over the ridge to Tamarack Lake, which lies less than 0.25 mile from Upper Twin Lake. Tamarack Lake reigns as the largest lake in the basin, and has the best views of the surrounding mountains. The lake's one major drawback is accessibility by 4-wheel drive vehicles (by going left at the fork 1.0 mile below the trailhead), which often means hikers must put up with several groups of campers and their attendant noise and clutter. Still, the lake definitely warrants a visit.

The meadows and ridge above Tamarack Lake make a great side hike. Follow the trail through the campsites on the eastern shore, then go up to the meadows southeast of the lake, where you'll find a small creek. Then use the scant trail to get up to the ridge, which is composed of a fantastic assortment of multicolored metamorphic rocks. Hike west along this ridge through a variety of wildflowers, and occasionally over pine mat manzanita. After 0.5 mile you'll reach the top of the 6,600-foot-high peak that towers above Upper Twin Lake. From here you'll have unimpeded views of Castle Crags, Grey Rocks, Flume Creek Ridge, and Mount Eddy to the north, the Trinity Alps to the west, Shasta Bally, Bully Choop, and the Sacramento Valley to the south, the mountains on the other side of I-5 to the east, and the three lakes below. Bring binoculars.

CHAPTER TWO
· · · · · · · · · ·
Shasta Lake National
Recreation Area

All the trails in this chapter run entirely or partially along Shasta Lake's shore. The Centimudi (hike 12), Dry Fork (hike 13), Bailey Cove (hike 16), and Hirz Bay trails (hike 18) remain within 100 yards of the high-water level for their entire distance; so in addition to open views of the surrounding mountains, you'll have the lake close by for swimming. The Clikapudi Trail (hike 14), which passes by Wintu Indian historical sites, offers a mix of lakeside walking and hiking in hills covered with pine and oaks. The Sugarloaf Trail (hike 17), the most strenuous and the most secluded, begins near the lake's shore and heads upstream along Sugarloaf Creek. The Samwel Cave Nature Trail (hike 19), which starts far up on the lake's McCloud arm, lets you explore a limestone cave and learn fascinating aspects of Wintu Indian and natural history. All of the trails are generally well defined and easy to follow, though occasionally intruded by poison oak.

Shasta Lake reigns as the dominant body of water in Northern California. Its 370 miles of shoreline encompass a 30,000-acre surface area and hold the waters of three major rivers: the Sacramento, the McCloud, and the Pit. Shasta Lake has also become a major tourist attraction, drawing visitors from all over who enjoy hiking, swimming, picnicking, fishing, sailing, houseboating, and water skiing.

The mountains surrounding the lake represent the southeastern boundary of the Klamath plate. The Klamaths, once part of the Sierra Nevada, split off about 140 million years ago and drifted northwest. The Cascades and Sacramento Valley filled the gap.

Massive gray limestone outcroppings provide welcome visual relief to the surrounding forested slopes on the east side of the McCloud River arm. Limestone is comprised of the compressed skeletal remnants of animals that lived in an ancient sea covering this region 200–300 million years ago. Water circulating through the easily dissolved limestone created Shasta Caverns. The Samwel Cave Trail takes you to a similar though less well-known cave. Other caves may exist in the area, but don't have a surface opening to facilitate their discovery.

The region's major tree and shrub species belong to the foothill and ponderosa-pine plant communities. Foothill species, such as digger pine, interior live oak, and whiteleaf manzanita, flourish at both lower elevations and in drier, exposed areas. Ponderosa pine and associated brethren, such as Douglas fir and black oak, dominate at higher elevations and on cooler, moister, north-facing slopes.

Wildlife abounds at Shasta Lake. Common mammals include deer, gray squirrels, and black bear. Scrub and Steller's jays scream loudly from the trees, making them the most noticeable of the many bird species that call Shasta Lake home. Keep your eyes open for the relatively rare osprey and bald eagle, which both compete with humans for the lake's fish.

The Wintu Indians originally inhabited the land under and around Shasta

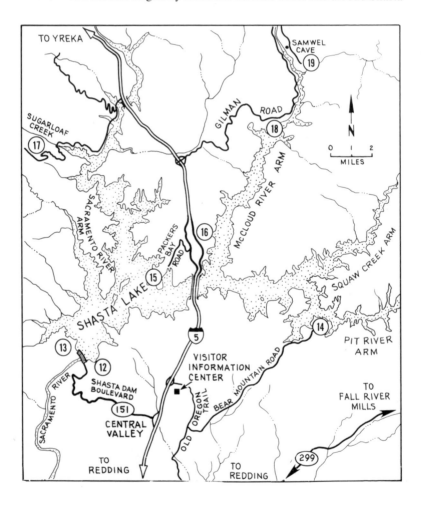

The three Shastas: Shasta Dam, Shasta Lake, and Mount Shasta.

Lake, often dwelling by the banks of the now-flooded rivers. As with other Native American tribes throughout California and the United States, they were forced off their land by the influx of miners and settlers.

Beginning in the 1850s, prospectors combed the hills and mountains in search of gold, but by the turn of the century mining efforts focused on copper. Large towns erupted near the copper mines: Kennett, just north of Shasta Dam, had 10,000 residents. However, sulphur fumes and other toxic substances from the copper smelters killed most vegetation for many miles in all directions. The resultant outrage from surrounding communities, combined with falling copper prices, forced the mines to close, and the towns died with them. Evidence of the environmental damage remains. In some areas relatively short trees comprise forests that sprouted only after the mines closed. And patches of bare soil mar mountainsides, the result of over seventy years of erosion.

The 1945 completion of Shasta Dam and subsequent filling of the lake flooded the decaying remnants of Kennett and similar towns, as well as Wintu Indian homes and settlers' ranches. The dam, which measures 602 feet high and 3,460 feet long, has two main purposes. First, it generates electricity by allowing the lake's water to flow through turbines. Second, it anchors the Central Valley Project: Shasta Lake (and other reservoirs such as Trinity and Whiskeytown lakes) stores water for use in irrigating crops in the Sacramento and San Joaquin valleys during the dry summer months. In addition, by regulating water flow, the dam ameliorates winter flooding and also helps repel San Francisco Bay salt water from the delta, thus protecting fresh-water species sensitive to high salinity.

The dam's Visitor's Information Center is open 9:00 A.M. to 4:00 P.M. every day in summer and Monday through Friday in winter. Interpretive photographic displays describe the history of the small towns under the lake and the building of the dam. Call (916) 275-4463 for more information.

The main Visitor's Information Center for the entire Shasta Lake National Recreation Area can direct you to one of the sixteen campgrounds (fee required) and provide you with informative brochures about local human and natural history. To reach the Visitor's Information Center, take the Mountain Gate exit off I-5 4.0 miles north of Redding, go to the east side of the freeway, then head south 100 yards on Holiday Road. It's open 8:30 A.M. to 4:30 P.M., Monday through Sunday in summer and 8:30 A.M. to 4:00 P.M., Monday through Friday in winter, though these hours may change.

· ·

12 CENTIMUDI TRAIL/SHASTA DAM

Jurisdiction and information: Visitor's Information Center, Shasta Lake Ranger District, 14250 Holiday Road, Redding, CA 96003. (916) 275-1589.
Length: 0.5 mile one way
Difficulty: Easy
Starting point: 1,070 feet
High point: 1,070 feet
Trail characteristics: Centimudi Trail is good packed dirt; all other walking is on pavement and concrete
Uses: Hiking, biking
Season: Year-round
Facilities: Bathrooms at the Shasta Dam Visitor's Information Center and at the Centimudi trailhead
Water: Available from drinking fountains
Map: USGS Redding

Walking in this area combines a demonstration of the power of man to alter his environment, as evidenced by the construction of Shasta Dam and the large amount of land flooded by Shasta Lake, with a bit of nature obtained from the Centimudi Trail along the lake's shore. Mount Shasta, the lake, and the surrounding mountains make for scenic views, and are nearly always visible.

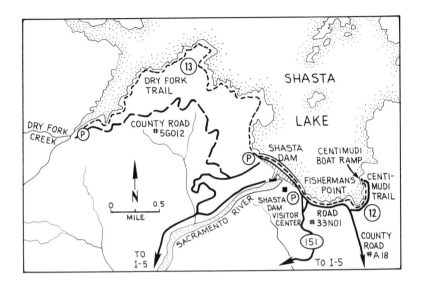

Take the Central Valley/Shasta Dam exit off I-5 4 miles north of Redding. Drive Route 151 (Shasta Dam Boulevard) through the dam construction towns of Project City, Central Valley, and Summit City for 3.0 miles to a four-way stop at Lake Boulevard. Continue straight for the scenic route to the dam. A vista point near the dam has great views of the three Shastas: Shasta Dam, Shasta Lake, and Mount Shasta. Shasta Dam is about 7 miles from I-5. Park in the dam's Visitor's Information Center lot (open 6:00 A.M. to 10:00 P.M.) or at the Fisherman's Point Picnic Area.

The 0.5-mile-long Centimudi Trail begins at the Fisherman's Point Picnic Area just east of the dam, and ends at the Centimudi boat ramp. Walk down the steps from the bathrooms; a sign points out the trailhead. The flat path passes by black oak, interior live oak, toyon, and whiteleaf manzanita. Several small trails allow easy access to the lake for swimming and fishing. Taking the uphill path at all forks will keep you on the main trail.

Many locals like to walk the 0.7-mile length of the dam. From the south side you can look down over the smooth slope of massive concrete and see the resurgent Sacramento River over 600 feet below. The north side gives views of fishermen, houseboats, and waterskiers. Near the west side the skeletal remnants of a 466-foot-high construction tower loom up from the lake's surface.

Those who wish more nearby hiking should see the Dry Fork Trail (hike 13) entry. Also, following the paved road west past the dam will eventually bring you to a dirt road that goes south along the river. Few cars drive this bumpy, lumpy road, making it more attractive to walkers.

· ·

13 DRY FORK TRAIL

Jurisdiction and information: Visitor's Information Center, Shasta Lake
Ranger District, 14250 Holiday Road, Redding, CA, 96003. (916) 275-
1589.
Length: 4.7 miles one way to Dry Fork Creek
Difficulty: Moderate
Starting point: 1,070 feet
High point: 1,120 feet
Trail characteristics: Dirt trail; easy walking
Uses: Hiking. Mountainbikes and horses can go the first 2.5 miles to where
the trail makes a narrow traverse of a steep cliff
Season: Year-round
Facilities: None
Water: None, bring your own
Map: USGS Redding

The Dry Fork Trail provides exquisite views of Mount Shasta, Shasta
Lake, and the surrounding mountains. It's primarily used by fishermen,
and there are many access points down to the lake's surface. Since the trail
follows the shoreline for almost its entire length, you'll see and hear the
fishermen on the shore and the many types of boats that take advantage of
the lake's recreational opportunities.

Take the Central Valley/Shasta Dam exit off I-5 4 miles north of Redding. Drive Route 151 (Shasta Dam Boulevard) for 3 miles to a four-way
stop sign at Lake Boulevard. Turn right or go straight: both ways lead to
Shasta Dam. Turn right on the first dirt road on the far side (west side) of
the dam. The last 200 yards to the trailhead are very rough, so you may
want to park by the dam. The signed trail begins at the high-water mark
just west of the parking area. If you have two vehicles and want to make a
one-way hike, drive to the trail's end by taking the unsigned dirt road located on the right 0.3 mile past the dam. It's 2.8 miles to Dry Fork Creek.
The trail ends between two redbud bushes 150 feet before crossing Dry
Fork Creek. There is room on the shoulder for several cars to park.

The trail winds in and out of small valleys that host equally small creeks
during the rainy season. In these valleys thrive plant species that require a
lot of water, such as willows, cottonwoods, ailanthus, wild grapes, and
blackberry bushes. On the hillsides, ponderosa pine and whiteleaf manzanita predominate, although there is the occasional Douglas fir or knobcone
pine.

Note that there are no trees over 50–60 feet in height. Sulphur fumes
from copper smelters in such towns as Kennett (400 feet under water just
north of the dam) killed most of the Shasta Lake region's vegetation in the

One of the many views of Shasta Lake from the Dry Fork Trail

early twentieth century. What you see has grown since the smelters were shut down for economic and environmental reasons in the 1920s. Once the vegetation was gone, soil erosion became a big problem. In an attempt to ameliorate this, metal grills were placed across the worst areas. If you look carefully you should see several of these during the course of your hike.

• •

14   CLIKAPUDI TRAIL

Jurisdiction and information: Visitor's Information Center, Shasta Lake
  Ranger District, 14250 Holiday Road, Redding, CA 96003. (916) 275-1589.
Length: 6.6-mile loop
Difficulty: Moderate
Starting point: 1,100 feet
High point: 1,300 feet
Trail characteristics: Dirt path is wide, gently sloped; easy walking
Uses: Hiking, mountainbiking, horseback riding
Season: Year-round
Facilities: Flush toilets near the trailhead
Water: Available from a drinking fountain near the trailhead, none along the
  trail
Map: USGS Millville

Ghosts from a time long past share the Clikapudi Trail with hikers. The
Wintu Indians lived in and around the area circumscribed by the trail, and
fenced-off archaeological sites and flat clearings whisper of more tranquil
days along Clikapudi Creek, before the white man's arrival.

This is one of the nicest hikes at Shasta Lake. Various vista points offer
views of the steep, forested slopes that surround the lake, and many
stretches of the trail leave twentieth century noise and bustle far behind.

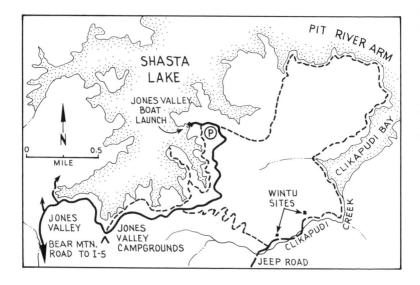

There are two ways to reach the trailhead. The first: take the Mountain Gate exit off I-5 north of Redding, drive east and south on Old Oregon Trail about 4 miles, then turn left onto Bear Mountain Road. Follow this road about 6 miles, then go right at the "Y" onto Jones Valley Road, which ends 2 miles farther at the Jones Valley boat launch. The trailhead is located just behind the large sign as you enter the boat-launch parking lot. The second: take Highway 299 east from I-5 about 6 miles to the town of Bella Vista, then turn left (north) onto Dry Creek Road. This road meets Bear Mountain Road 4 miles later, just before Jones Valley Road.

The trail begins in an unusually large knobcone pine forest, which stretches southwest all the way to the lower Jones Valley Campground. But it quickly abandons these strange trees with their tightly attached cones for more common ponderosa pines, interior live oaks, and whiteleaf manzanita.

After surmounting a saddle, the way drops down to the lake's high-water line. At this point, 1.0 mile from the trailhead, the Pit River arm opens up to full view. When the lake is low you'll see the bleached corpses of trees sticking straight out of the water. Most vegetation below shoreline was removed before the dam was completed, but America's 1941 entry into World War II meant manpower could not be spared to clear trees on the upper stretches of the Pit River. Today these denuded snags provide valuable habitat for bass and other fish.

The trail undulates along the Pit River arm for another 0.5 mile, then turns southwest to follow Clikapudi Bay. Over the next mile the path passes by a manzanita-enshrouded picnic table, over a small wooden bridge, through a thick grove of Douglas fir, then turns west to follow the part of Clikapudi Creek not captured by the lake.

After a 0.5-mile walk through the creek's flat valley, you'll see an area on the right surrounded by a high barbed-wire fence. It's the first protected Wintu site; the second fenced site is 0.25 mile farther down the dirt road. No obvious physical evidence manifests the past activities of the Wintu, so you'll have to use your imagination.

The trail along Clikapudi Creek intermingles with a 4-wheel-drive road; from the first fenced site on, take the dirt road farthest north and closest to the sites, following it past the second site as it climbs northwest out of the valley and narrows back to trail.

From the saddle above Jones Valley Road, 0.5 mile from the second site, switch back down to the pavement, cross the road, and head right 50 yards to the signed continuation of the trail. The path continues its descent another 0.2 mile to a trail fork. The left (west) trail ends after 1.0 mile at the lower Jones Valley Campground. The main trail continues right (east) through the knobcone pine forest for 1.3 miles back to the trailhead. One-half mile past the fork is a short, unmaintained trail on the left that follows a hillside finger down to the lake's shore. It allows a shortcut straight to the parking lot when the lake level is low.

15 WATERS GULCH TRAILS

Jurisdiction and information: Visitor's Information Center, Shasta Lake
   Ranger District, 14250 Holiday Road, Redding, CA 96003. (916) 275-1589.
Length: 2.5 miles one way to Packers Bay boat ramp
Difficulty: Moderate
Starting point: 1,250 feet
Low point: 1,070 feet
Trail characteristics: Easy walking on a wide, gently sloping path
Uses: Hiking, mountainbiking, horseback riding
Season: Year-round
Facilities: Flush toilets located at Packers Bay boat ramp, 0.5 miles down the
   road from the trailhead
Water: Available at Packers Bay boat ramp, and from Waters Gulch Creek
   through midsummer
Map: USGS Lamoine

Solitude, a shaded creek, and views of the lake and surrounding mountains greet hikers on the Waters Gulch Trail. A small swimming hole on Waters Gulch Creek and several access points to the lake make summer swimming easy and pleasant.

Take the Packers Bay exit off I-5 15 miles north of Redding and 3 miles north of the bridge across Shasta Lake. Go under the freeway, and get on I-5 south. Get off 1.0 mile later at the Packers Bay exit. Turn right, and go approximately 1.0 mile, then turn right into a small paved parking lot on the right-hand side. The trail leaves from this lot.

Two trails leave from the parking lot, both signed. The first, the Overlook Trail, gains 200 feet of elevation over 0.4 mile while gently climbing under black oak and ponderosa pine. At the overlook, digger pine, interior live oak, and whiteleaf manzanita predominate. Two benches allow you to rest and enjoy the scenery. The lower one gives views to the west and southwest. You can see the lake, the mountains beyond, and even the top of Shasta Bally, just west of Whiskeytown Lake. From the upper bench you can see Packers Bay and the mountains to the south.

The Waters Gulch Trail, the main trail here, also leaves from the trailhead. It starts out fairly level along the north side of the hill. The black oaks, young Douglas firs, and big-leaf maples along this stretch thrive in the wetter, cooler climate found on the north sides of mountains and hills.

The trail descends gradually over the first 0.4 mile, then meets the cool environs of Waters Gulch Creek, which is shaded by dogwood, canyon live oak, and Douglas fir. Notice the thick grapevines hanging down from the canyon live oaks.

After you hike 500 yards farther, your ears will let you know there is cascading water nearby, then your eyes will confirm it. A series of pools and small waterfalls delights the senses, with the largest pool inviting you for a dip on hot days. Please don't try to make your way down from this point: you'll cause significant erosion damage to the trail and hillside. Instead, follow the trail down about 200 yards, where you'll see a bench on the right-hand side. From this bench go straight and a little right to make your way down to the creek. Getting to the falls and pools will require some scrambling and rock hopping, but a scant and intermittent trail will help. The rock-ringed swimming hole nestles between short waterfalls, and although relatively small, offers enough room to cool off. At a minimum, you can admire the rushing water and relax under the shade of white alder and canyon live oak.

Back on the main trail, you'll follow a mostly level course near the lakeshore. About 0.5 mile from the swimming hole the trail switches back away from the lake and climbs in an easterly direction. Another 0.5 mile farther the trail goes along a ridge shaded by black oaks, where the author for several minutes observed an oblivious black bear snuffling about in the thick mat of fallen leaves.

After passing through a saddle, the trail gently descends 0.7 mile on the

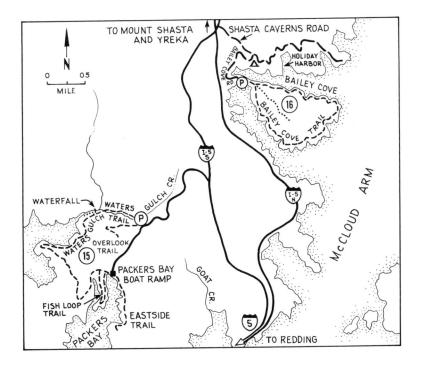

south side of the mountain through drier, more exposed terrain to the Packers Bay boat ramp parking lot. From here you can either return the way you came, or hike up the road 0.5 mile to your car.

There are two other small trails nearby, neither very spectacular. To hike the 0.7-mile-long Fish Loop Trail, go 100 yards down the Waters Gulch Trail from the northwest end of the Packers Bay boat ramp parking lot. The signed, relatively level trail heads south along the east side of a seasonal creek under black and live oak, and comes to an overlook point after 500 yards. From here one has access to the lake for fishing and swimming. The trail then returns on the other side of the small ridge in full view of the boat ramp, then ends at the southwest corner of the parking lot.

The 0.25-mile-long Eastside Trail leaves the east side of the boat ramp by a sign saying "docking access," and is marked by a hiker symbol. Flat, a little brushy, and somewhat exposed, it ends at a bench with an open view of the lake and marina. You can easily scramble down the lake's red shores for a swim.

16 BAILEY COVE TRAIL

Jurisdiction and information: Visitor's Information Center, Shasta Lake
   Ranger District, 14250 Holiday Road, Redding, CA 96003. (916) 275-1589.
Length: 2.8-mile loop
Difficulty: Easy
Starting point: 1,100 feet
High point: 1,150 feet
Trail characteristics: Dirt trail is generally easy to walk on; a few slippery
   spots
Uses: Hiking, mountainbiking, horseback riding
Season: Year-round
Facilities: Toilets and picnic tables near the trailhead
Water: Available from drinking fountains near the trailhead
Map: USGS Lamoine

Bailey Cove offers a wide variety of recreation options, and is a great destination for the whole family. Shaded picnic tables sit near the lake's shore, and the water beckons both swimmers and boaters. Of course, the preferred option is hiking.

Take the Shasta Caverns Road exit off I-5 about 15 miles north of Redding, then head east, following signs for Shasta Caverns. After 0.4 mile, turn right onto Bailey Cove Road. This road ends 0.7 mile later at the boat

Canyon live oaks at the Bailey Cove trailhead

launch, which is where you should park.

The signed trail starts at the eastern edge of the picnic area, and is described here from a counterclockwise perspective. The gently undulating path begins under the shade of canyon live oaks, then over the next mile encounters a grove of big-leaf maples festooned with hanging wild grapevines, a small band of buckeye trees, and a group of knobcone pines with hundreds of pine cones tightly glued to trunks and branches.

After passing several small springs, the trail leaves the distant noise of the freeway behind. To the east, the lake's blue waters reflect the huge slabs of gray limestone that house Shasta Caverns.

Just past the half-way point the vegetation begins to change. Douglas fir, ponderosa pine, and black oak thrive in the shadier conditions on the north side of the mountain. As you walk back to the parking area under the shade of these towering trees, Holiday Harbor's houseboat heaven floats serenely in the cove on the right.

If you want to do some climbing, head up the unmarked trail located between the two ends of the Bailey Cove Trail loop at the picnic area. It reaches the summit of the hill in 0.5 mile or so, but the way becomes steadily more difficult to follow, necessitating some bushwhacking near the top. The scenery isn't as good as one would expect: black oaks and digger pines effectively block most views.

. . . .

17 SUGARLOAF CREEK TRAIL

Jurisdiction and information: Visitor's Information Center, Shasta Lake
  Ranger District, 14250 Holiday Road, Redding, CA 96003. (916) 275-1589.
Length: Up to 3.0 miles one way
Difficulty: Moderate
Starting point: 1,150 feet
High point: 1,950 feet
Trail characteristics: The trail, unmaintained in recent years, is covered with
  leaves and pine needles, and some stretches are composed of loose
  rock. There are also several short, steep sections.
Uses: Hiking
Season: Year-round
Facilities: None
Water: Available year-round from Sugarloaf Creek and its tributaries
Map: USGS Lamoine

Remoteness and lush creek-side vegetation lure hikers to Sugarloaf Creek. The one significant disadvantage is the physical state of the trail itself: you'll have to pay so much attention to making out the trail and keeping your feet on it that you can only view the surrounding scenery when you stop.

Sugarloaf Creek runs year-round, and originates a few miles northwest of the trailhead. The trail itself parallels the creek, and always stays on the north side. If you hike on a hot day be sure to take note of the swimming hole just south of where Lakeshore Drive crosses the creek. If you're will-

Lush foliage shades the cool waters of Sugarloaf Creek. (photo by Rick Ramos)

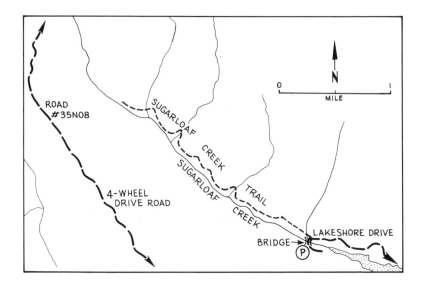

ing to search, you can find a few smaller swimming spots farther upstream.

Take the Lakeshore exit off I-5 about 25 miles north of Redding. Go under the freeway and turn left onto Lakeshore Drive. After 6.0 miles the pavement ends; the remaining 0.7 mile to Sugarloaf Creek is good dirt road. Park near the road on the north side of the creek, or down by the creek itself on the south side.

The unsigned trail begins from the road on the north side of the bridge. The first 0.5 mile travels through relatively open territory, with good views of the steep, heavily forested mountains. This is also the driest part of the hike: notice the digger pines and interior live oaks on the south-facing slope to your right.

As the trail continues its undulating uphill course, it passes through vegetation composed of species that thrive in a moister, shadier habitat. Towering Douglas firs stretch far above, and canyon live oaks, ranging in size from the small and ordinary to the huge and twisted, are everywhere. Bigleaf maples and dogwood, the most numerous deciduous trees, provide dazzling colors in autumn.

The trail itself is usually well above Sugarloaf Creek, and nears it only at a few points. It does cross four small, year-round tributary creeks, which can serve as both sources of drinking water and cool, shaded resting spots.

As you progress up the trail, it gradually fades. Once it went all the way up to a dirt road on the ridge, but time has taken its toll and it now dissipates into several small game trails after encountering a large fallen tree. You can continue farther by following the game trails and going cross-country.

• • • • • • • • • • • • • • • • • • • •

18 HIRZ BAY TRAIL

Jurisdiction and information: Visitor's Information Center, Shasta Lake
  Ranger District, 14250 Holiday Road, Redding, CA 96003. (916) 275-1589.
Length: 1.6 miles
Difficulty: Easy
Starting point: 1,100 feet
High point: 1,150 feet
Trail characteristics: Gently sloping dirt path; easy walking
Uses: Hiking, mountainbiking, horseback riding
Season: Year-round
Facilities: Bathrooms at Hirz Bay Campground and Dekkas Rock Picnic Area,
  picnic tables at Dekkas Rock Picnic Area
Water: Available at Hirz Bay Campground and Dekkas Rock Picnic Area
Maps: USGS Lamoine and USGS Bollibokka Mountain

This trail offers good views of Shasta Lake and the mountains that border
its southern shore, and also winds through three small valleys that host
three small creeks, all with wooden bridges.

Take I-5 north of Redding 20 miles to the Gilman Road exit. Go east on
Gilman Road 10 miles, then turn right into the Dekkas Rock Picnic Area.
The signed trail begins on the right.

The trail is described here as beginning at Dekkas Rock Picnic Area because of a lack of parking places at the Hirz Bay Campground, combined
with the requirement to pay the camping fee just to get in. For those al-

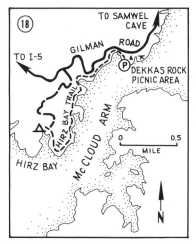
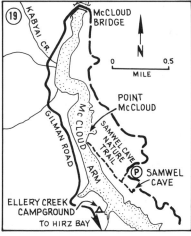

ready camping at Hirz Bay, the signed trail begins by campsite 47.

From Dekkas Rock the trail undulates along the McCloud Arm lakeshore, encountering the first of the three small creeks 300 yards from the trailhead. Guarded by numerous canyon live oaks, this creek ranks as the smallest.

For the next 0.5 mile the trail passes through outcroppings of limestone, the remains of marine animals deposited 200–300 million years ago on ancient seabeds, since compressed into the gray rock you see around you.

Big-leaf maple, canyon live oak, dogwood, and grapevine-covered Douglas fir amply shade the second creek, located nearly 1.0 mile from the trailhead. A wooden bench makes this a great place to rest and enjoy the scenery.

Farther on down the trail another bench faces a huge canyon live oak that's 5 feet in diameter with several main trunks. Just beyond, a stand of particularly tall ponderosa pines stretches into the sky.

You'll encounter the last creek, the nicest of the three, about 1.4 miles from the trailhead. Autumn enhances its beauty: the leaves of big-leaf maple and dogwood turn to vibrant yellows, pinks, and reds.

The trail passes through another stand of tall ponderosa pines just before entering the Hirz Bay Campground. Look towards the lake at this point and you'll see several knobcone pines, distinguished by numerous cones tightly bound to trunks and branches.

• •

19   SAMWEL CAVE NATURE TRAIL

Jurisdiction and information: Visitor's Information Center, Shasta Lake
   Ranger District, 14250 Holiday Road, Redding, CA 96003. (916) 275-1589.
Length: 0.7 mile one way
Difficulty: Moderate
Starting point: 1,350 feet
Low point: 1,050 feet
Trail characteristics: Leaf- and needle-covered trail in relatively good shape,
   but steep and slippery from the cave up to the parking area
Uses: Hiking, mountainbiking, horseback riding
Season: Year-round
Facilities: None
Water: None
Map: USGS Bollibokka Mountain

Samwel Cave highlights this hike. Long a Wintu Indian spiritual center, visiting shamans sought magical powers in its deep, dark pools, and incorporated the chamber's mystical aura into medicinal herbal mixtures.

Waters of an ancient sea covered this area 200–300 million years ago. Pressure slowly compressed marine animal shells to limestone over the aeons, and now this gray-colored rock extrudes from mountainsides in the region surrounding Samwel Cave. Limestone is easily eroded by water. Samwel Cave, like nearby Shasta Caverns and many other caves, was formed over millions of years by the circulation of underground water.

Take I-5 north of Redding 20 miles to the Gilman Road exit. Go east on Gilman Road 16 miles to the McCloud River Bridge, after which the paved road turns to gravel. Continue 2.2 miles past the bridge, where you'll see two successive ridges on the right with places to park. Park at the second ridge, located about 100 yards past the first. There is no sign. An alternative way to get to the cave is to boat up the McCloud River arm of Shasta Lake to Point McCloud, which is 0.5 mile past the Ellery Creek Campground. Head southeast up an old dirt road to the trail. This second alternative is limited to periods when the lake is nearly full.

An interpretive 0.5-mile trail leads from near Point McCloud at the lake's edge up to the cave. Its signs describe many Wintu legends, and also the first visit by a white man in 1903. They are meant to be read in order, with the last signs in the cave itself.

However, most people will begin from Gilman Road, where a short, steep trail connects with the interpretive trail just before the cave. Ideally you should head down to the interpretive trail's beginning in order to read the signs on the way up, but you will no doubt want to see the cave first, so follow the trail's contour around the mountain to the cave's entrance.

The cave's roomy first chamber is easily accessible, averaging head height, and requires neither a flashlight nor special equipment. Sufficient sunlight enters to illuminate the surreal colors of the pink, purple, green, and blue-gray minerals precipitated on the walls and ceiling.

Signs describe the wealth of anthropological and zoological specimens found within the far reaches of the cave. These include ancient human artifacts predating the arrival of the Wintu, and the skeletal remains of extinct animal species such as the short-faced bear, ground sloth, and shrub oxen. Also, the discovery of relatively recent human remains in a deep pit gives credence to the Wintu legend of the lost Indian maiden. The young woman supposedly fell while seeking the magical waters of one of the pools.

A locked gate near the cave's floor on the far wall guards Samwel Cave's extensive interior network of passages, pools, and pits. If you are an aspiring or experienced spelunker who would like to explore the deep, dark recesses of the cave, contact the Shasta Lake Ranger District for information regarding safety and obtaining a gate key.

After exploring the cave, head down the interpretive trail, realizing, of course, that you are doing it backwards as far as the signs are concerned. The trail ends at an old dirt road, which you can follow down to the banks of the McCloud arm.

CHAPTER THREE
• • • • • • • • • • •
Whiskeytown National Recreation Area

The trails in this chapter offer a variety of hiking options. The Davis Gulch Trail (hike 29), which runs near the lake's shore, has markers that introduce you to most of the region's major plant species and allows easy lake access for swimming on warm summer days. Other trails that travel by the lake are the Shasta Divide Nature Trail (hike 20), which also instructs you on local natural history, and the Great Water Ditch Trail South (hike 27). The Tower House Historic District Trails (hikes 22–23) go through an area rich in local history, as does the Mount Shasta Mine Loop Trail (hike 26). The Mill Creek (hike 23), Boulder Creek (hike 25), Clear Creek (hike 28), and Lower and Upper Brandy Creek trails (hikes 30–31) all travel near year-round streams that boast small waterfalls and numerous swimming holes.

The trails vary from the wide and flat to the narrow and steep. Be on the look-out for poison oak, which often grows next to and even in many of the less-traveled trails. All major trails are included here, but dozens of dirt-roads and fragments of old trails crisscross the entire park, and many of these make good side trips.

The Visitor's Information Center, located 6 miles west of Redding at the intersection of Highway 299 and Kennedy Memorial Drive, has numerous brochures on local natural history and recreation opportunities. It's open daily from Memorial Day to Labor Day; hours vary other times of the year. Park headquarters, located 0.5 mile down Kennedy Memorial Drive from Highway 299, is open daily year-round from 8:00 A.M. to 4:30 P.M. and is another excellent source of information and brochures. The headquarters phone number is (916) 241-6584.

There are three camping options. Oak Bottom (fee required), 5 miles west of the Visitor's Information Center on Highway 299, has 105 walk-in tent sites and 50 RV sites. Brandy Creek (fee required), 4.5 miles down Kennedy Memorial Drive, has 37 RV sites. Backcountry camping, allowed in regions 1.0 mile or more from the lake, requires a permit. These free permits are available at park headquarters.

Whiskeytown Lake is the crown jewel of the Central Valley Water Project's many reservoirs. Its clear waters reflect the forested slopes of the steep surrounding mountains and provide a perfect foreground for the imposing visage of 6,209-foot-high Shasta Bally, the dominant peak of the region. The combination of this spectacular beauty and a wide variety of recreational opportunities, such as swimming, fishing, sailing, canoeing, and water skiing, draws visitors from across the country.

The area under and around the lake has historically been the center of much human activity. The Wintu Indians and other tribes originally inhabited the area: evidence of campsites dates back 4,000 years. These Native Americans lived in harmony with nature's cycles, gaining sustenance by gathering acorns and other fruits of native plants, catching salmon, and hunting deer, antelope, and elk.

The discovery of gold in Clear Creek in 1848 changed the Wintus forever. Miners drove the Indians from their land, and more than 70 percent died from disease or violent confrontations with whites.

The miners quickly spread throughout the region, initially searching the

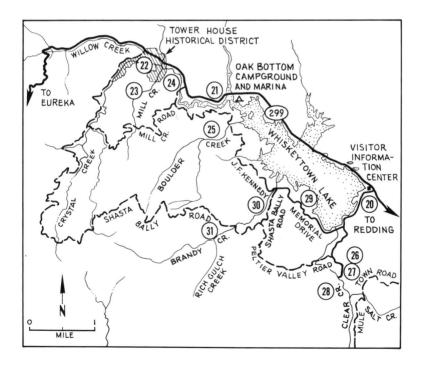

A young hiker inspects a tombstone along the Camden Water Ditch Trail (hike 22).

sand and gravel of stream bottoms for the precious yellow metal. However, this easily accessible gold quickly played out, and more technologically sophisticated, and environmentally destructive, methods were developed. Shafts dug deep into mountainsides gave access to veins of rock relatively rich in gold. Stamp mills used heavy weights to crush the rock to powder, after which mercury was used to pull out the gold. Piles of rock and ore tailings still dot the mountainsides.

By the 1920s most mines had stopped operation, and the population of Whiskeytown, the lake's namesake which boasted more than 1,000 residents during the Gold Rush heyday, shrunk considerably.

However, the construction of Whiskeytown Dam ensured the town's demise. Begun in 1959 and completed in 1963, the dam and lake comprise an integral part of the Central Valley Water Project. Water released from the lake irrigates crops in the Sacramento and San Joaquin valleys.

Although the dam impounds the water of Clear Creek and other smaller streams, it also holds water that is diverted through 11 miles of tunnels from Lewiston Lake in Trinity County. This diversion allows the generation of electricity at Carr Powerhouse and provides more water for the Central Valley.

While the Whiskeytown Lake area is rich in human history, it also offers much to those interested in natural history. The mountains surrounding the lake make up the southeastern edge of the Klamath Mountains. Shasta Bally is a partially exposed, decaying granite batholith that formed many millions of years ago from cooling underground magma. Many streams throughout the region have cut down to the underlying granite, so you'll often see granite boulders in the water and near the banks.

As with nearby Shasta Lake, the Whiskeytown area hosts plants from the foothill woodland and ponderosa pine plant communities. Foothill woodland species, generally found at lower elevations and in drier spots such as exposed south-facing slopes, include interior live oak, digger pine, and whiteleaf manzanita. Ponderosa pine species thrive at higher elevations and in the cooler, shadier areas of lower elevations. Common representatives include black oak, ponderosa pine, Douglas fir, and white fir.

A variety of wildlife inhabits the region, though you'll probably need to hike away from the heavily visited areas to see the rarer and shyer species. Look for gray squirrels, chipmunks, and mule deer. Black bears roam the forest, and occasionally visit campgrounds and picnic sites in search of food. More than one hundred different species of birds, including the bald eagle, either live here year-round or are seasonal visitors.

· ·

20 SHASTA DIVIDE NATURE TRAIL

Jurisdiction and information: Park Headquarters, Whiskeytown National Recreation Area, P.O. Box 188, Whiskeytown, CA 96095. (916) 241-6584.
Length: 0.25 mile one way to the lake
Difficulty: Easy to moderate
Starting point: 1,380 feet
Low point: 1,210 feet
Trail characteristics: Sloping dirt path can be slippery in places
Uses: Hiking
Season: Year-round
Facilities: Bathrooms and information at the Visitor's Information Center
Water: Available from a drinking fountain at the Visitor's Information Center
Map: USGS French Gulch

The Shasta Divide Nature Trail provides a good introduction to the Whiskeytown National Recreation Area. In addition to dazzling views of the lake and surrounding mountains, you'll see, and learn to identify, many of

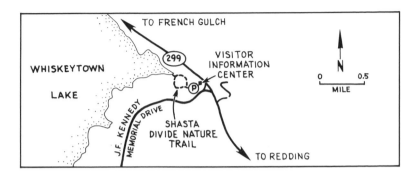

the major local plant species. The trail has twelve numbered posts, each by a different plant. A free brochure describing the plants is available inside the Visitor's Information Center and at the trailhead.

The trail begins at the southwest corner of the Visitor's Information Center parking lot. As you descend the trail towards the lake, you'll encounter poison oak at the first post. Note the characteristic three-leaf arrangement of the leaves. The shapes of the leaves themselves can vary, and the body of the plant can vary from a shrub to a vine, but this three-leaf arrangement always remains the same. Avoid touching poison oak; it contains oils that can irritate the skin and cause severe rashes.

When you have gone past posts 2 through 4 (California buckeye, California black oak, and toyon, respectively) go left at the fork in the trail. At post 5 is a young incense cedar, which appears to be nearly dead. The trail then goes by a small creek, where you'll see wild grapevines hanging from a canyon live oak at post 6. At post 7 is the whiteleaf manzanita. Another species of manzanita, greenleaf manzanita, has dark green leaves. Though less abundant than its relative which you see before you, it thrives in many areas around Whiskeytown Lake.

The trail then goes down by the lakeshore, where you'll find an excellent spot to swim and enjoy the beautiful view of the lake. You'll also find posts 8 and 9, which mark knobcone pine and white alder.

The trail then begins to climb back up towards the parking lot. At post 10 you'll see a digger pine. This tree is a rare example of its species because it has only one trunk and that trunk has grown relatively straight. "Diggers" usually have several main trunks which twist and turn in all directions, providing an endless variety of shapes to stimulate the imagination.

Post 11 supposedly represents mistletoe. However, the mistletoe has either died or been removed.

At post 12 is interior live oak, a common tree of the Northern California foothills. Two hundred feet farther up the trail you'll reach a fork in the trail. The uphill path leads back to the trailhead.

21 GREAT WATER DITCH TRAIL NORTH

Jurisdiction and information: Park Headquarters, Whiskeytown National
  Recreation Area, P.O. Box 188, Whiskeytown, CA 96095. (916) 241-6584.
Length: 2.5 miles one way
Difficulty: Easy to moderate
Starting point: 1,220 feet
High point: 1,260 feet
Trail characteristics: Generally good, but with some rocky and slippery
  areas, and several short stretches of steep trail
Uses: Hiking, mountainbiking
Season: Year-round
Facilities: Bathrooms, cold showers, and food at Oak Bottom
Water: Available at Oak Bottom
Map: USGS French Gulch

This hike, one of the easiest in the park, follows a section of the Great Water Ditch, which stretched a total of 41 miles and provided water for mining
operations over a century ago. The generally wide and flat trail makes an
excellent outing for a family with children. Ample shade and proximity to

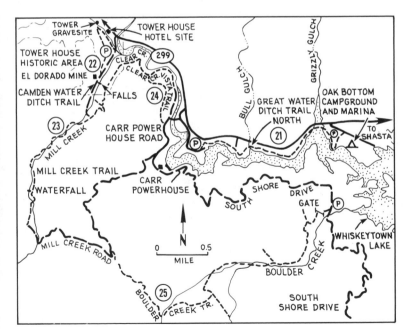

The Great Water Ditch Trail North offers open views of Whiskeytown Lake and Shasta Bally.

the lake offer respite from summer heat, and you'll often have open views of the water and mountains.

A wide variety of plant life grows along the trail. Near the lake and small seasonal streams you'll see water-loving plants such as alders, blackberries, and ferns. Digger and knobcone pines, copious quantities of manzanita, and several species of oak populate the drier areas.

Head west on Highway 299 for 5 miles past the Visitor's Information Center, then turn left at Oak Bottom. Follow the road for 200 yards, then park at the wide area on the right. The trail is described here as beginning from Oak Bottom. However, it can just as easily be reached from the other end by taking the first left off Carr Powerhouse Road. This paved road, an old section of Highway 299, ends after 1.5 miles at a large parking lot. The trail, marked by a hiker sign, begins at the northeast corner of the parking lot.

To begin the hike from the Oak Bottom parking area, look for the sign that says "jogging trail." (There are several fitness exercises you can do in this area of Oak Bottom.) Follow the trail down to the lake. The trail runs for 0.5 mile along the lakeshore, then goes beside Highway 299. Thankfully, it leaves the highway for good 300 yards farther to follow the Great Water Ditch. About 1.5 miles from the beginning of the trail you'll come to a rickety log bridge that will require some care in crossing. A locked gate 200 yards farther presents little difficulty for hikers, but bikers must lift their bikes over it. After another 200 yards you'll cross a wide dirt road, and 0.5 mile later you'll reach the end of the trail.

• •

22 CAMDEN WATER DITCH TRAIL TO EL DORADO MINE

Jurisdiction and information: Park Headquarters, Whiskeytown National
   Recreation Area, P.O. Box 188, Whiskeytown, CA 96095. (916) 241-6584.
Length: 1.4-mile loop
Difficulty: Easy
Starting point: 1,220 feet
High point: 1,280 feet
Trail characteristics: Sandy in some places, but generally good walking
Uses: Hiking, mountainbiking
Season: Year-round
Facilities: Outhouse at trailhead
Water: Available year-round from Willow Creek
Map: USGS French Gulch

This hike offers a wide variety of plant life, ranging from riparian habitat to open meadows to towering Douglas firs and ponderosa pines. Also, the historic old buildings, water ditches, and abandoned mines are reminders of the area's rich human history. A brochure available from a box at the trailhead explains these relics in detail.

Take Highway 299 west past the Visitor's Information Center and Oak Bottom. About 8 miles past the Visitor's Information Center, and 1.3 miles past the turnoff to Carr Powerhouse, you'll see a "County Park" sign. Turn left and follow the dirt road down to the parking area, which is near the confluence of Willow Creek and Clear Creek.

To begin the hike, cross the Willow Creek Bridge and turn right. The wide sandy trail initially follows Willow Creek, where willows, cottonwoods, and white alders grow in abundance. The grassy meadow on the left erupts with wildflowers every spring. The burial site of Levi Tower lies 0.25 mile from the trailhead. Several incense cedar trees shade the grave and its surrounding white picket fence.

The trail meets the Camden Water Ditch just past the Tower grave site. Turn left to go to the El Dorado Mine. The trail also extends to the right, but poison oak, blackberry vines, and other bushes quickly overgrow it.

The trail then offers open views of the Tower House Historical District as it runs under the shade of canyon live oaks, black oaks, and Douglas firs. The Tower House Historic District encompasses much of the land and buildings owned by two of the area's earliest pioneers: Levi Tower and Charles Camden. They came to Shasta County to seek their fortune mining gold, but quickly turned to more lucrative pursuits. Tower built his "Tower House" hotel here in the 1850s. He used much of the surrounding fertile meadows to grow fruit and vegetables and raise livestock to feed his guests. The hotel burned down in 1919 and its exact location is now unknown.

Camden built all the buildings still standing, including the large Camden House near the parking lot. Nearby structures include a carriage house and a storage building. A tenant caretaker house and a large barn are located across the meadow near the site of Camden's sawmill. About 0.25 mile from the grave site the trail joins a dirt road. Turn right on this road and follow it for 250 yards under tall ponderosa pines to the El Dorado Mine.

The gold mine, in operation as late as the 1960s, has many interesting features. You can see the old stamp mill, and behind it the mineshaft going back into the hill. An old ore cart sits forlornly on metal tracks at the shaft's mouth.

If you wish to extend your hike, continue up the dirt road past the mine to the Mill Creek and Clear Creek Vista trails (hikes 23 and 24).

To return to the trailhead, follow the dirt road down to the Willow Creek bridge. Along the way back you'll pass the site of the Camden Sawmill, the tenant farmhouse, and the large old barn.

Hikers prepare to enter the cool recesses of the El Dorado Mine.

23　MILL CREEK TRAIL

Jurisdiction and information: Park Headquarters, Whiskeytown National
　Recreation Area, P.O. Box 188, Whiskeytown, CA 96095. (916) 241-6584.
Length: 2.4 miles one way to Mill Creek Road
Difficulty: Moderate
Starting point: 1,220 feet
High point: 2,050 feet
Trail characteristics: Gently climbing trail's surface varies from sand to
　packed clay to rock; there are nineteen creek crossings
Uses: Hiking, horseback riding
Season: Year-round
Facilities: Outhouse at trailhead
Water: Available from Mill Creek
Map: USGS French Gulch

This hike is one of the best in the Whiskeytown National Recreation Area.
The trail goes through the Tower House Historical District and by the El
Dorado Mine. However, once past the mine it leaves all sights and sounds

A hiker soaks her feet in Mill Creek's soothing waters.

of civilization behind as it follows Mill Creek, a cool, clear, year-round stream where foot-long fish swim in the deeper pools. You'll hike in shade almost the entire time, and two swimming holes make this hike especially attractive on hot summer days.

Plant life abounds. Huge Douglas firs and ponderosa pines stretch into the sky, and canyon live oaks, big-leaf maples, and white alders thrive in the damp, shaded soil near the stream. At higher elevations dogwood trees provide a beautiful display of large white flowers in spring and vibrantly colored leaves in autumn.

However, there are certain dues that must be paid by those who wish to enjoy this beauty. For starters, the trail crosses the creek nineteen times. Wet feet are a distinct possibility in winter and spring when the water-flow rate peaks. Also, the trail occasionally fades to the point of disappearing. However, red ribbons tied to trees and shrubs at a height of 6 feet help guide you. Stay alert and you'll have no problems following the trail.

Take Highway 299 west past the Visitor's Information Center and Oak Bottom. About 8 miles past the Visitor's Information Center, and 1.3 miles past the turnoff to Carr Powerhouse, you'll see a "County Park" sign. Turn left and follow the dirt road down to the parking area, which is near the confluence of Willow Creek and Clear Creek.

To begin the hike, cross the Willow Creek Bridge and follow the dirt road through the meadow and on to the El Dorado Mine. Be sure to investigate the mine if you haven't already done so on a previous visit.

One hundred yards past the mine you'll hear the sound of a little waterfall. Your ears will guide you to the right spot, where you'll also find an attractive swimming hole. Though not large, it's big enough and deep enough for a refreshing dip.

One-quarter mile past the mine the road crosses the creek at a grassy area. Continue on the trail, which is marked by hiker and equestrian signs. Another 0.25 mile past these signs large grapevines drape down to the ground from numerous ponderosa pines, some from heights as high as 50 feet. Three hundred yards farther down the trail a huge incense cedar tree soars skyward. Note the scratch marks at the base of the trunk; these are probably the work of bears.

The second, and best, swimming hole on Mill Creek lies 1.3 miles past the El Dorado Mine. Fed by a 5-foot waterfall, it measures 15 feet around and 5 feet deep. This is an excellent spot at which to cool off and rest.

One hundred feet farther the trail turns 90 degrees to the left. After walking by dogwood trees for 200 yards, you'll cross Mill Creek. The trail follows one of Mill Creek's tributary streams for awhile, then climbs steeply up a ridge. The trail becomes a dirt road the last 50 yards, then ends where it intersects Mill Creek Road.

If you wish to extend your hike, walk in either direction along Mill Creek Road, which sees very little traffic. If you head east (left) for 1.0 mile you'll reach the Boulder Creek Trail (hike 25).

. . . .

24 CLEAR CREEK VISTA TRAIL

Jurisdiction and information: Park Headquarters, Whiskeytown National
   Recreation Area, P.O. Box 188, Whiskeytown, CA 96095. (916) 241-6584.
Length: 4.2–5.0 miles round-trip, depending on trail options selected
Difficulty: Moderate
Starting point: 1,220 feet
High point: 1,520 feet
Trail characteristics: Wide dirt trail, occasionally intruded by easily avoided
   poison oak
Uses: Hiking, mountainbiking, horseback riding
Season: Year-round
Facilities: Outhouse at trailhead
Water: Available year-round from Mill Creek and Clear Creek
Map: USGS French Gulch

This intermediate distance hike provides good views of the Tower House
Historic District, Clear Creek, and the surrounding mountains. It also offers several optional side hikes.

Take Highway 299 west past the Visitor's Information Center and Oak
Bottom. About 8 miles past the Visitor's Information Center, and 1.3 miles
past the turnoff to Carr Powerhouse, you'll see a "County Park" sign.
Turn left and follow the dirt road down to the parking area, which is near
the confluence of Willow Creek and Clear Creek.

To begin the hike, cross the Willow Creek Bridge and follow the dirt
road 0.4 mile past the old barn and tenant farmer house to the El Dorado
Mine. Then proceed 250 yards farther to trail fork marked by a hiker symbol, where you'll turn left and cross the creek. As you go up the steps on
the other side, you'll notice an old rusted bed and other artifacts. At one
time this might have been a gold miner's cabin site.

The trail leads uphill through ponderosa pine, Douglas firs, and various
oaks. About 100 vertical feet above Mill Creek it nears some powerlines.
Turn left (north) and follow the flat trail, which was probably a water ditch
in the past. (The trail to the right, a pleasant detour, passes by some beautiful small streams which flow down moss-covered rocks. It's intruded by
brush in many areas, and ends after 1.0 mile at Mill Creek.)

A few hundred yards farther along on the main trail an old, closed-off
mineshaft disappears into the hillside. One hundred yards past this
mineshaft are the remains of a tree fort in a canyon live oak. This section of
the trail allows open views of Shasta Bally and the surrounding region.

About 1.0 mile from where the Clear Creek Vista Trail leaves Mill
Creek you'll meet an old dirt road. Follow this road uphill for 100 feet,
where the trail resumes on the left. The trail drops a few feet, then heads

A young woman boulder-hops across Mill Creek at the beginning of the Clear Creek Vista Trail.

east under the comforting shade of over-arching canyon live oaks and black oaks.

Four hundred yards past the above-mentioned dirt road you'll reach a fork in the trail. You have three options.

Option One: Take the left fork. This trail winds gently downhill until it reaches Clear Creek, where you can observe the various willows, alders, cottonwoods, and associated shrubs and grasses that comprise riparian habitat. A side trail accesses the creek itself, where you can swim on warm days.

One-half mile from the fork in the trail is a dirt road with a circular turn-around area, which is the end of the trail. From here you can either return the way you came or follow Option Three.

Option Two: Take the right fork of the trail. It traverses along the mountain side, staying level except for a few undulations. After several hundred yards it leaves the trees for more open terrain. Shasta Bally looms directly ahead, and the blue expanse of Whiskeytown Lake lies to the east.

The trail eventually drops down to Carr Powerhouse Road. Two faint trail fragments intersect the main trail over the last 200 yards. Bear left at all intersections and continue downhill. It's 0.75 mile between the trail fork and the road.

Option Three: You can make a loop by combining options one and two. From the Option One end proceed 300 yards east along the dirt road to Carr Powerhouse Road. Then turn right and go 600 yards down towards the powerhouse. You'll then see a large digger pine on your left and the trail leading uphill to your right.

From the Option Two end you must reverse this process. After reaching Carr Powerhouse Road turn left and follow it for 600 yards. Then turn left again at the dirt road just before the bridge. Proceed down the road 300 yards to the circle turnaround, where you'll see the trail.

25 BOULDER CREEK TRAIL

Jurisdiction and information: Park Headquarters, Whiskeytown National Recreation Area, P.O. Box 188, Whiskeytown, CA 96095. (916) 241-6584.
Length: 3.1 miles one way to Mill Creek Road
Difficulty: Moderate
Starting point: 1,300 feet
High point: 2,250 feet
Trail characteristics: Wide, gently climbing trail; easy walking
Uses: Hiking, mountainbiking, horseback riding
Season: Year-round
Facilities: None
Water: Available from Boulder Creek
Map: USGS French Gulch

This trail has several advantages: it's wide enough for two people to walk abreast; the 1,100 total feet of climbing is evenly spaced throughout the 3.1 miles to Mill Creek Road; towering ponderosa pines, Douglas firs, and canyon live oaks provide ample shade for more than half the trail's length; occasional vista points offer expansive views of Shasta Bally, Whiskeytown Lake, and the surrounding forested mountains; and finally, you'll enjoy the beauty of the many shades of lush green that contrast with the granite boulders and clear rushing waters of Boulder Creek.

Squirrels are common inhabitants of the forests around Whiskeytown Lake.

Drive west on Highway 299 2 miles past Oak Bottom and turn left on Carr Powerhouse Road. Three-tenths of a mile past the powerhouse itself turn left onto dirt South Shore Drive. Two and a half miles farther is a crossroads, where you'll see a sign with the hiker and equestrian symbols. The Boulder Creek Trail begins as the road to your right, which heads west. For those who wish to come from Brandy Creek, follow the main paved road northwest 1.4 miles, then turn left onto the dirt South Shore Drive. Follow this road for nearly 3.0 miles until you reach the above-mentioned crossroads. The trail begins on your left.

To begin the hike, head west up the dirt road through the gate (which may or may not be closed). After 500 yards of gentle climbing go left at a fork in the road. About 1.0 mile from the trailhead you'll come to yet another fork—turn left and cross Boulder Creek for the first time.

Lush vegetation highlights the next 0.75 mile: grapevines hang from tall Douglas firs, maples spread their broad leaves to catch the sunlight filtering through the branches of taller trees, and ferns grow in abundance in cool, shaded areas. After twice crossing Boulder Creek during this particularly beautiful stretch, the trail widens and heads uphill through more open country.

Two miles from the trailhead, and 0.25 mile past the most recent creek crossing, the trail forks once again. Turn right and follow the main trail uphill. One-half mile later you'll cross Boulder Creek for the last time, then climb 1.0 mile more up to where the trail meets Mill Creek Road. This is a good spot to rest and enjoy the views of forested slopes and deep valleys.

Afterwards, you can retrace your steps back to the trailhead or extend your hike by heading west (left) on Mill Creek Road. If you wish, you can walk about 1.0 mile west on Mill Creek Road to where the Mill Creek Trail comes in on the right. You can then hike down this beautiful trail to the Tower House Historic District.

26 MOUNT SHASTA MINE LOOP TRAIL

Jurisdiction and information: Park Headquarters, Whiskeytown National Recreation Area, P.O. Box 188, Whiskeytown, CA 96095. (916) 241-6584.
Length: 3.0-mile loop
Difficulty: Moderate
Starting point: 1,100 feet
High point: 1,650 feet
Trail characteristics: Generally easy walking, except for a few steep parts that can be slippery
Uses: Hiking, mountainbiking, horseback riding
Season: Year-round
Facilities: None
Water: Available from Orofino Creek through midsummer
Map: USGS French Gulch

The Mount Shasta Mine Loop Trail is a good mid-distance hike that offers a combination of mining history, creek-side scenery, and good views of the surrounding mountains. Be warned that much of the trail is exposed to the sun, so avoid it during the hot summer months.

From the Visitor's Information Center at Highway 299, take Kennedy Memorial Drive. Bear left at the dam onto Paige Bar Road. After 1.0 mile you'll see a sign for the trail. Park in the large lot on the left.

You can hike the loop in either direction, but it's described here from a counterclockwise perspective. To begin, go to the signed trailhead at the southeast corner of the parking lot. After 0.25 mile you'll see the Whiskeytown Cemetery, which was moved here before the lake covered the old site. The trail parallels Paige Bar Road for a few hundred more yards, then heads east. Six-tenths of a mile from the trailhead the unmarked Great Water Ditch Trail South (hike 27) leaves on the right.

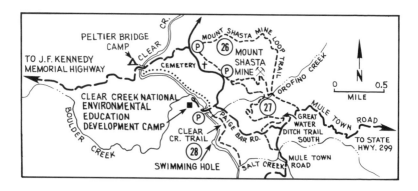

You'll then walk through a large, dense grove of knobcone pines. These trees only sprout after a fire, so some time in the not-too-distant past a major conflagration must have swept through this area.

The Mount Shasta Mine lies 1.1 miles from the trailhead. During its heyday at the turn of the century it was the most productive in the Shasta mining region. A fence blocks access to the 465-foot-deep main shaft. Several large canyon live oaks make this a pleasant spot, and the area immediately surrounding the mine merits exploration.

The trail briefly goes alongside a seasonal creek, then follows Orofino Creek 100 yards upstream. Here a spur trail on the right goes past several mineshafts to Mule Town Road, which is 400 yards away. The main trail climbs up alongside Orofino Creek for 0.4 mile, where you'll see mine tailings and rock retaining walls. It then leaves the creek to make a steep climb north up to a ridge.

Open views of Shasta Bally, Whiskeytown Lake, and the dam make the climbing effort worthwhile. Close by you'll notice many tall, strangely twisted digger pines. The trail now heads left (west), following an old dirt road along the ridge. It's an easy 0.8 mile walk downhill past knobcone pines and black oaks to the trailhead.

· ·

27 GREAT WATER DITCH TRAIL SOUTH

Jurisdiction and information: Park Headquarters, Whiskeytown National
    Recreation Area, P.O. Box 188, Whiskeytown, CA 96095. (916) 241-6584.
Length: 2.5 miles one way
Difficulty: Easy to moderate
Starting point: 1,060 feet
Low point: 1,000 feet
Trail characteristics: Generally flat trail has two steep sections; poison oak
    intrudes in many areas
Uses: Hiking, mountainbiking, horseback riding
Season: Year-round
Facilities: None
Water: Available through midsummer from Orofino Creek
Map: USGS French Gulch

This trail follows the same water ditch described in the Great Water Ditch Trail North (hike 21) entry. The ditch, in use over a century ago, provided mining operations a constant supply of water. The hike itself travels mainly through groves of oak and pine, and offers few expansive views.

From the Visitor's Information Center at Highway 299, take Kennedy

Memorial Drive. Bear left at the dam onto Paige Bar Road. Go 1.5 miles, then park by four large boulders on the left.

To get to the trailhead, walk past the boulders and turn right onto the Mount Shasta Mine Loop Trail (hike 26). After 200 yards you'll see a clearing on the right where an unusually large knobcone pine is located by the side of the trail. About 100 feet past this clearing, and up a little incline, the unsigned Great Water Ditch Trail South heads south on the right.

One-half mile from the trailhead, the trail leaves the nearly flat water ditch and makes a steep descent to Orofino Creek. A small tributary stream to Orofino Creek makes a nice spring side hike: follow the scant trail 100 yards upstream to the small waterfall and its surrounding blanket of wildflowers.

After heading downstream for 0.5 mile, the trail leaves the Orofino Creek drainage, then gently twists for 1.0 mile until it meets Paige Bar Road. It resumes on the other side of the road, where it's marked by a horseback riding sign. After traveling 200 yards under dense trees it descends 100 feet down to its end at Mule Town Road.

· ·

28 CLEAR CREEK TRAIL

Jurisdiction and information: Park Headquarters, Whiskeytown National Recreation Area, P.O. Box 188, Whiskeytown, CA 96095. (916) 241-6584.
Length: 1.0 mile one way to Salt Creek
Difficulty: Moderate
Starting point: 950 feet
Low point: 800 feet
Trail characteristics: Wide, sandy dirt trail offers mostly easy walking, but is steep and slippery in spots
Uses: Hiking, mountainbiking, horseback riding
Season: Year-round
Facilities: None
Water: Available from Clear Creek, but bring your own; creek water could have contaminants from Whiskeytown Lake
Map: USGS French Gulch

This trail offers one of the best hikes at Whiskeytown. Clear Creek is the main attraction: its waters spurt from the bottom of Whiskeytown Lake through the dam's turbines, then flow through a rocky canyon to eventual confluence with the Sacramento River just south of Redding. The cold water harbors fish that lure both human anglers and great blue herons. At the trailhead you'll find a breathtaking view of Shasta Bally and South Fork Mountain, both mirrored in the momentarily calm water of a cattail and willow-ringed widening of the creek.

From the Visitor's Information Center at Highway 299, take Kennedy Memorial Drive. Bear left at the dam onto Paige Bar Road. Follow signs for NEED Camp, and park on the right just before crossing the bridge over Clear Creek. The parking area is 3 miles from Highway 299.

The trail begins by a hiker symbol on the south side of the road. It immediately crosses Orofino Creek, then makes a steep ascent. Your vigorous climb reaps the reward of viewing the creek rushing far below and 2,616-foot-high Kanaka Peak looming on the far side. If you look carefully, you may see some burned understory vegetation from the 1990 Kanaka Fire.

One-half mile from the trailhead the path descends near Clear Creek. Make the short scramble down to the best swimming hole in the region: a 10-foot-deep, rock-walled pool of summer refreshment that measures 100 feet by 30 feet. After steeping yourself in the beauty of this spot, continue on the trail as it parallels Clear Creek's downstream direction. After passing a mineshaft, you'll travel through a mixed forest of black oak and knobcone pine. About 1.0 mile from the trailhead the path drops precipitously down to the creek, where an old rock wall testifies to past human activities, most likely gold mining. Salt Creek ends its brief journey here, and a short rock hop up the seasonal stream reveals a small, cool, peaceful wading pool shaded by vertical rock cliffs.

On your way back you may want to take some of the faint side trails that issue periodically on both sides of the trail. A couple go down to Clear Creek; others head towards Paige Bar Road.

There are additional hiking options from the parking area. You can hike south cross-country along the creek, and there are several short paths just to the north. A rough, 1.0-mile-long fisherman's trail runs alongside the creek north of the bridge, and ends at Peltier Bridge Camp. Hiking it involves scrambling over large rocks and performing similar feats of moderate agility.

Yerba santa grows in dry areas around Whiskeytown Lake.

29 DAVIS GULCH TRAIL

Jurisdiction and information: Park Headquarters, Whiskeytown National
  Recreation Area, P.O. Box 188, Whiskeytown, CA 96095. (916) 241-6584.
Length: 3.3 miles one way to the Brandy Creek Picnic Area
Difficulty: Moderate
Starting point: 1,300 feet
Low point: 1,210 feet
Trail characteristics: Generally easy walking on packed clay; a few steeper
  areas are a bit slippery
Uses: Hiking
Season: Year-round
Facilities: None at trailhead; toilets are located at Brandy Creek Picnic Area,
  but may be closed in winter months; swimming area has showers and
  food for sale during summer
Water: Available from drinking fountains at the Brandy Creek Picnic Area;
  bring your own
Map: USGS French Gulch

The Davis Gulch Trail, designed especially for hikers, is one of the most
accessible trails in the Whiskeytown National Recreation Area. A dozen
benches along the trail provide comfortable resting spots, and trailside

*A sign at the Brandy Creek Picnic Area shows the Davis Gulch Trail and Whis-
keytown Lake.*

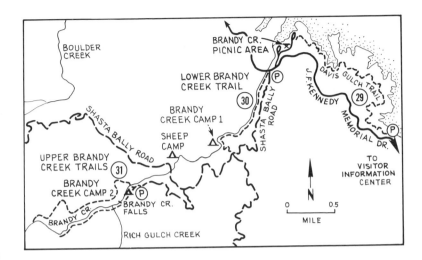

plaques describe seventeen plant species found throughout the region. Towering stands of ponderosa pine shade the trail in late afternoon and early evening, and make for a relatively cool hike when hot weather sets in. It isn't necessary to hike the trail's entire length: you'll find most of the plant identification plaques within the first 2.0 miles, along with the best views and swimming spots.

From the Visitor's Information Center at Highway 299, take Kennedy Memorial Drive. The signed trailhead is on the right, 0.7 mile past the dam's far end.

A sign directs you to the trail's beginning. The path winds in and out of small shaded canyons that sport small gurgling streams in winter and spring. A little over 2.0 miles from the trailhead, the path descends to the lakeshore. The beautiful secluded cove on the right invites you for a swim on warm days. If you look carefully at the trail's left side, you'll see the remains of old mine shafts that have been filled in with dirt.

The trail then continues its generally northwesterly course, staying close to the lakeshore for the next 0.5 mile. Finally it climbs gently up to a ridge, then descends to the east parking lot of the Brandy Creek Picnic Area. Just to the north is the old boat-launching area, closed since the opening of the marina on the next cove over. If it's summertime, you can wander over to the main swimming area and get something to eat from the snackbar. Be warned that everything shuts down for winter.

You can just as well hike the Davis Gulch Trail from the Brandy Creek end, a good idea if you're already picnicking there with friends or family. A 0.5-mile walk along the trail will bring you to the lakeshore. There you can enjoy the cool water in relative peace, far from the crowds packing the main swimming areas.

· ·

30 LOWER BRANDY CREEK TRAIL

Jurisdiction and information: Park Headquarters, Whiskeytown National
   Recreation Area, P.O. Box 188, Whiskeytown, CA 96095. (916) 241-6584.
Length: 1.1 miles to Brandy Creek Camp 1
Difficulty: Moderate
Starting point: 1,250 feet
High point: 1,650 feet
Trail characteristics: Varies from a wide dirt road to a leaf-strewn, brush-
   intruded narrow path
Uses: Hiking, mountainbiking, horseback riding
Season: Year-round
Facilities: None
Water: Available from Brandy Creek
Map: USGS French Gulch

This trail closely parallels Brandy Creek, and provides numerous views of
clear water cascading over granite boulders and streaming through stands
of canyon live oak and white alder to the lake. The trail quality varies
widely. White and orange ribbons help you through the difficult spots, and
staying near the creek will always keep you on the right path.

    From the Visitor's Information Center on Highway 299, take Kennedy

Knobcone pine: note the cones tightly bound to the trunk and branches.

A hiker attempts to cross swift-flowing Brandy Creek.

Memorial Drive 4.5 miles to Brandy Creek. Park on the left at the small picnic area just before the bridge.

A hiker symbol at the picnic area marks the beginning of the trail. The way gently climbs through a mixed forest of ponderosa pine, Douglas fir, and the occasional incense cedar or knobcone pine, with the soothing song of the creek constantly in your ears. You'll discover many places to get down to the creek's banks and also several swimming areas. The steep mountains that border Brandy Creek limit scenic vistas, but you'll catch a few glimpses of South Fork Mountain.

Almost 1.0 mile from the trailhead the path narrows, then begins a sharp ascent to the campsites of Brandy Creek Camp 1. If you wish to make a loop hike, continue up the dirt road for 300 yards to the main Shasta Bally Road, then follow it downhill to the parking area. You can also follow this same road uphill 2.2 miles to the beginning of the Upper Brandy Creek Trails (hike 31).

. . . .

31 UPPER BRANDY CREEK TRAILS

Jurisdiction and information: Park Headquarters, Whiskeytown National Recreation Area, P.O. Box 188, Whiskeytown, CA 96095. (916) 241-6584.
Length: Varies from 200 yards to 2.0 miles one way
Difficulty: Easy to moderate, for all trails
Elevation gain: All 3 trails begin at 2,000 feet. The Brandy Creek Falls Trail ends at 2,050 feet, the south trail ends at 2,400 feet, and the north trail ends at 2,650 feet
Trail characteristics: Generally easy walking, but steep, sandy sections can be slippery
Uses: Hiking, mountainbiking, horseback riding
Season: Year-round
Facilities: None
Water: Available from Brandy Creek and other year-round and seasonal streams
Map: USGS French Gulch

The clear, cold waters of Brandy Creek originate on the upper slopes of Shasta Bally and South Fork Mountain, and gather into an impressive roar as they cascade in numerous waterfalls down to an eventual rendezvous with Whiskeytown Lake. However, the still waters of deep swimming holes occasionally contrast the thunder of the creek's rush through the canyon. These pools intermingle the verdant shades of stream-side vegetation with the whitish-gray of granite boulders and sand.

Few people frequent these trails, so you should have this beautiful territory all to yourself. Summer is a particularly good time to visit: the cool night air lingers in the canyon near the creek, and ample shade and numerous swimming spots bring additional relief on even the hottest day.

Near water, and in shaded areas on slopes, you'll see canyon live oak, white and red alder, big-leaf maple, and some dogwood. In other areas you'll encounter ponderosa pine, Douglas fir, black oak, and whiteleaf manzanita. You should also find a few sugar pines: their characteristic foot-long cones droop from the ends of upper branches and also lie scattered about the surrounding forest floor.

From the Visitor's Information Center at Highway 299, take Kennedy Memorial Drive 4.5 miles to Brandy Creek. Turn left onto Shasta Bally Road 100 yards past the entrance to Brandy Creek Marina. The pavement quickly turns to dirt as you progress uphill. One and two-tenths miles after leaving the main road, go straight at a three-way fork, then left 1.0 mile later at another fork. One mile past this second fork is the Brandy Creek Camp 2 campsite on the right. Park here. (Small waterfalls interspersed between great swimming holes are just down the steep, short path from the parking area.)

There are three trails. The shortest, at only 200 yards, is the Brandy Creek Falls Trail. Leave the parking area and follow the road uphill. One hundred feet before Brandy Creek you'll spot a faint, narrow trail marked by yellow ribbons. After skirting through bushes and past steep slopes, it ends at a spectacular 25-foot-high, two-tiered waterfall with a good swimming hole at its base.

The 1.6-mile-long south trail begins on the left as you head up the road from the parking area towards Brandy Creek. It has an inauspicious start: keep your eye peeled for its unsigned beginning. However, it quickly becomes a good trail as it closely parallels Brandy Creek's south bank. Nearly 0.5 mile from the road it crosses Rich Gulch Creek, which originates high up on the slopes of South Fork Mountain. As you continue ever uphill, note that the trail itself slopes into the side of the mountain. It's probably an old water ditch from days long past, most likely constructed by gold miners. After passing several springs and small seasonal creeks it ends in an area of unsurpassed beauty for this region. Several sequential waterfalls dominate the landscape as their waters course over smooth granite. Numerous pools are interspersed throughout, and the imposing presence of dozens of massive canyon live oaks completes the scene.

The 2.0-mile-long north trail, the unmaintained continuation of the main road, is marked with a hiker symbol. It meanders in a generally upstream direction after crossing Brandy Creek, and climbs almost the whole way, usually out of sight of Brandy Creek far below. In several areas the vegetation opens up to reveal unimpeded views of Shasta Bally's slopes to the north, South Fork Mountain to the south, and the Brandy Creek canyon stretching west. The trail ends at its only meeting with the creek. The water spilling over granite boulders under the shade of red and white alders helps create a tranquil mood that's perfect for a relaxed picnic.

CHAPTER FOUR
• • • • • • • • • •

McArthur–Burney Falls Memorial State Park

McArthur–Burney Falls Memorial State Park is interlaced with numerous hiking trails. It also includes over 2 miles of stream frontage on Burney Creek, along with some shoreline on Lake Britton. You can fish for native and planted trout in the creek, and for bass, crappie, and catfish in the lake. In addition, swimming and boating are popular at the lake.

However, the park's crown jewel is Burney Falls itself. Two hundred million gallons of water a day cascade 129 feet into deep icy-blue pools, creating a sensory feast for the mind, body, and soul.

The Falls Trail (hike 32) takes you to the base and lip of the falls. The P.S.E.A. and Headwaters trails (hikes 33 and 35) both travel along Burney Creek: the shaded P.S.E.A. Trail downstream of the falls, the more exposed Headwaters Trail upstream. The Burney Creek Trail/Rim Trail Loop (hike 34) allows you to visit Lake Britton for a swim and then enjoy views of the Burney Creek canyon as you hike along the rim high above. The Pioneer Cemetery Trail (hike 36) visits a small, nineteenth century graveyard before ending at the shore of Lake Britton. Large signs near the overlook contain a park map, which includes all trails and also information on geology and fauna. All trails are signed, but be aware that the posted mileages are round-trip, not one way.

The park is located in the southern portion of the Cascade geological province, so volcanic action has played a dominant role. However, this action was not the violent eruptions of the type that formed Mount Lassen. Rather, liquid basalt oozed from fissures and shield volcanos, spread rapidly over large areas, and cooled in large slabs. As you hike, you'll see layers of this dark rock, each caused by different flows, with more recent flows overlying the older. The forces of wind, water, and gravity have caused some of these lava sheets to crack and fall from the canyon rim, so you'll see basaltic rocks of various sizes scattered throughout the park.

Nearer the creek, and prevalent in places around Lake Britton, are layers of diatomite interspersed between basalt. Diatomite, a powdery, cream-colored rock, consists of silica-containing, algae fossil shells deposited on the bottoms of ancient lakes.

Springs from a vast underground reservoir of water are the main source of Burney Creek and Burney Falls. These springs surface about 0.5 mile above the falls, and the creek stays bone-dry above this point during summer and early fall when rainfall is scarce. Since the water source is so large, the flow over Burney Falls remains relatively constant year-round.

The slow erosion of material under the top layers of basaltic rock created Burney Falls. Over a long period of time, the falls gradually retreated upstream to their present position. The continual process of erosion could cause a dramatic rockslide in the near future that would significantly alter the falls' appearance.

Even a casual inspection of Burney Falls reveals two distinct areas from which water flows. In addition to the main flow of water over the top of Burney Falls, underground water seeps through porous rock to emerge halfway down the face of the falls.

A wide variety of flora flourishes within the park boundaries. The major conifers are ponderosa pine, Douglas fir, and incense cedar. The two dominant oak species are California black oak and Oregon white oak. Along the banks of Burney Creek and Lake Britton you'll see white alder, dogwood, and vine maple. Together with Oregon ash, these deciduous trees provide a vibrant display of color in autumn. Major shrub species are greenleaf manzanita, flowering currant, and redbud. Also, various flowers bloom during the spring and summer months. Be sure to get the brochure for the nature trail; it points out many of the species mentioned above, in addition to providing other interesting information about the region's geology.

Squirrels and chipmunks have no problems overcoming shyness, and you'll see them throughout the park. You can also expect to see other species of animals common to ponderosa pine habitat, such as black-tail deer, though these are often frightened away by the large numbers of people in the park. However, there always seems to be a Steller's jay within earshot, if not eyeshot. You may see several different species of water birds at Lake Britton, and, if you're lucky, a bald eagle.

A Native American tribe, the Ilmawi, originally inhabited the area around Burney Falls. Whites called them the Pit River Indians because of their practice of digging large pits in which to trap game animals. The Ilmawi considered the falls a spiritual place.

In the second half of the nineteenth century, whites used this area for ranching and farming. The only productive soil for growing crops was near the Pit River, and so most farms were flooded when Lake Britton was created. Some of these settlers are buried in the Pioneer Cemetery (hike 36), which you can visit. Remember that it's forbidden to disturb any archaeological sites, whether Native American or pioneer.

Burney Falls: the waters of Burney Creek plunge 129 feet into a deep pool.

The park, open year-round, offers 128 campsites (fee required). Two excellent brochures, one on the park and one describing the numbered stops
on the interpretive nature trail, are available for a small fee from both the
check station and vending machines. There is also a park entrance fee.

32 FALLS TRAIL

Jurisdiction and information: McArthur–Burney Falls Memorial State Park, Box
  1260, Burney, CA 96013. (916) 335-2777.
Length: 1.0-mile loop
Difficulty: Easy to moderate
Starting point: 3,000 feet
Low point: 2,850 feet
Trail characteristics: The first part of the path is paved; the rest is dirt
Uses: Hiking
Season: Year-round
Facilities: Toilets and showers in the campground and near the park's main
  entrance
Water: Available from drinking fountains in the campground and near the
  Visitor's Information Center, and from Burney Creek
Map: USGS Ponderosa

This is the most popular trail in the park, and with good reason. The 1.0-mile loop encompasses some of the best scenery and offers close-up views of Burney Falls. Twenty-four numbered posts line the route, and the brochure available from both the check station and vending machines explains exactly what you'll see at each post.

From Redding, take Highway 299 about 60 miles east to the intersection with Highway 89. Take 89 north for 6 miles. Signs will direct you to the park. The parking lot lies near the check station.

The trail begins at the falls overlook. This is a good spot to take photos of the falls. As you continue along the trail be sure to stop frequently to look at the beautiful scenery.

As you gradually descend to the deep pools at the base of the falls, note how the air temperature drops. The water temperature averages 45 degrees, and its mist provides welcome relief on a hot summer day.

From the falls, continue downstream along Burney Creek. Just before crossing a footbridge you'll see the Burney Creek Trail (hike 34) continuing on downstream. Just past the bridge the P.S.E.A. Trail (hike 33) leaves on the right, also following the creek down to Lake Britton. Cross the bridge, head left, and climb up to another open view of the falls. The trail then continues upstream of the falls, where it crosses another footbridge. On the right just before the bridge is a faint fisherman's trail that closely hugs the stream bank for 0.25 mile. It's worth taking; it'll get you away from the crowds.

After crossing the footbridge, the trail comes back to the falls overlook. You can use the map and descriptions of other trails to plan side hikes from this central trail.

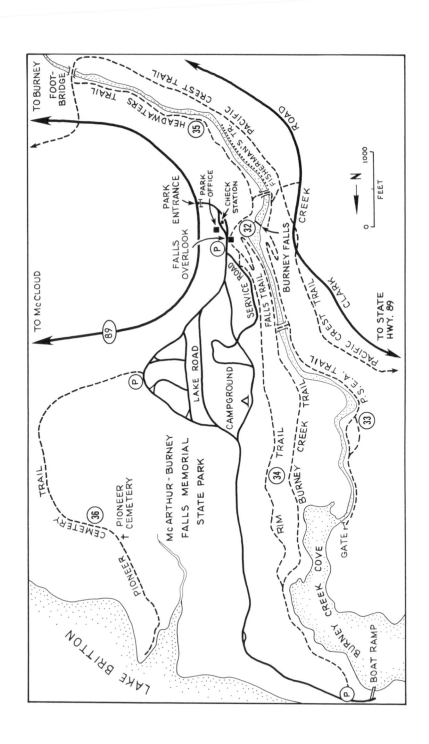

33 P.S.E.A. TRAIL

Jurisdiction and information: McArthur–Burney Falls Memorial State Park, Box 1260, Burney, CA 96013. (916) 335-2777.
Length: 0.5 mile one way
Difficulty: Easy
Starting point: 2,850 feet
High point: 2,875 feet
Trail characteristics: Mostly flat dirt path with some areas of powdery diatomite
Uses: Hiking
Season: Year-round
Facilities: Toilets and showers in the campground and near the park's main entrance
Water: Available from drinking fountains in the campground and near the Visitor's Information Center, and from Burney Creek
Map: USGS Ponderosa

This trail begins on the west side of the downstream footbridge of the Falls Trail (hike 32), about 0.5 mile from the falls overlook. The 0.5-mile route, amply shaded by Douglas fir, dogwood, and white alder, runs near the

Tiger lilies grow near the edge of Burney Creek.

edge of the stream the whole way. Vine maple grows in quantity here and provides a spectacular visual display in autumn.

After 0.25 mile you'll encounter an area of diatomite, which forms a fine, white powder on the trail. Near here is a quiet spot to sit by the creek and have a picnic lunch. Just beyond, the trail briefly splits, with the upper leg avoiding the dust of the lower leg.

The trail ends at a locked gate. This is also a good place to sit for awhile and enjoy the views of the mouth of Burney Creek, Lake Britton, and the mountain rim to the east.

34 BURNEY CREEK TRAIL/RIM TRAIL LOOP

Jurisdiction and information: McArthur–Burney Falls Memorial State Park, Box 1260, Burney, CA 96013. (916) 335-2777.
Length: 1.5 miles to the falls overlook
Difficulty: Easy to moderate
Starting point: 2,850 feet
High point: 3,000 feet
Trail characteristics: Dirt path with some powdery diatomite
Uses: Hiking
Season: Year-round
Facilities: Toilets and showers at Lake Britton, in the campground, and near the park's main entrance
Water: Available from drinking fountains at Lake Britton, in the campground and near the Visitor's Information Center, and from Burney Creek
Map: USGS Ponderosa

Although you could do the loop in either direction, it's described here as beginning at the east side of the downstream footbridge of the Falls Trail (hike 32), 0.5 mile from the falls overlook. It's about 1.5 miles to return to the overlook, with another 0.5 mile tacked on if you go down to Lake Britton.

The Burney Creek Trail's name is somewhat misleading. It follows the creek for only the first 100 yards, then never rejoins it. It initially goes along the base of the cliff. The basaltic rocks on the right fell from the rim high above to form talus.

The vegetation here differs from that encountered along the creek. The drier, warmer conditions exclude trees like white alder and dogwood. Here ponderosa pine, Douglas fir, incense cedar, the occasional white fir, black oak, and Oregon white oak predominate.

Basalt boulders flank the beginning of the Burney Creek Trail.

One-half mile from the trailhead, the route meets the shoreline of Lake Britton near the mouth of Burney Creek. Over the next 200 yards you'll walk by diatomite cliffs with the concomitant trail dust.

One-quarter mile past the diatomite cliffs you'll reach a fork in the trail. (If you have time, take the 0.3-mile-long trail to the left on down to Lake Britton, where you'll find a picnic area, sandy swimming beach, boat launch ramp, and views of the lake and surrounding mountains.)

From where the three trails meet, the Rim Trail goes right and climbs 200 feet over the next 0.3 mile to the rim of Burney Creek canyon, where you'll be treated to views of the creek and its streamside vegetation. Eventually the trail runs beside the campground, and finally ends near the falls overlook.

35 HEADWATERS TRAIL

Jurisdiction and information: McArthur–Burney Falls Memorial State Park, Box 1260, Burney, CA 96013. (916) 335-2777.
Length: 0.5 mile one way
Difficulty: Easy
Starting point: 3,000 feet
High point: 3,025 feet
Trail characteristics: Mostly flat dirt path
Uses: Hiking
Season: Year-round
Facilities: Toilets and showers in the campground and near the park's main entrance
Water: Available from drinking fountains in the park campground and near the main entrance, and from Burney Creek
Map: USGS Ponderosa

This trail follows Burney Creek upstream above the falls and offers good access to the creek for fishing. One drawback is the nearness of Highway 89; you'll definitely hear the traffic.

From Redding, take Highway 299 about 60 miles east to the intersection with Highway 89. Take 89 north for 6 miles. Signs will direct you to the park. The parking lot lies near the check station.

This trail leaves from the south side of a gravel parking lot located 200 yards south of the falls overlook. Note how the water velocity and volume decrease as you go upstream. Near the end of the trail, the creek dries up completely in summer and early fall because it's above the level of the springs that provide most of Burney Creek's water.

The Headwaters Trail merges with the Pacific Crest Trail (PCT) just before a footbridge across the creek. You can return to the trailhead by retracing your steps, or you can cross the bridge and follow this relatively mundane section of the PCT. After 0.7 mile it intersects a short trail that takes you to the upper footbridge of the Falls Trail (hike 32), just above the falls.

. . . .
36 PIONEER CEMETERY TRAIL

Jurisdiction and information: McArthur–Burney Falls Memorial State Park, Box 1260, Burney, CA 96013. (916) 335-2777.
Length: 1.0 mile one way to Lake Britton
Difficulty: Easy
Starting point: 3,000 feet
Low point: 2,800 feet
Trail characteristics: Old dirt road; easy walking
Uses: Hiking
Season: Year-round
Facilities: Toilets and showers in the campground and near the park's main entrance
Water: Available from a drinking fountain just across the road from the trailhead
Map: USGS Ponderosa

This trail, actually an old dirt road, travels through an open forest of ponderosa pine and incense cedar to the Pioneer Cemetery and Lake Britton. This whole area along the road was once the site of farming homesteads, and before that it was used by Native Americans. Remember not to disturb any sites of previous human activity, and don't remove any relics.

Drive highway 299 from Redding about 60 miles east to the intersection with Highway 89. Take 89 north for 6 miles. Signs will direct you to the park.

From the entrance to the campground, take successive right turns for 0.5 mile until you see a small parking area on the right. The trail begins by a nearby log. The dirt road makes a long, gradual curve over 0.75 mile, then comes to the Pioneer Cemetery. Feel free to observe the graves of the pioneers; many died before the beginning of the century. Most headstones are still legible. One marks the grave of a little girl who died at the age of four, another a sixteen-year-old boy who died in the middle of summer.

If you follow the road down another 0.25 mile you'll reach a relatively secluded area of Lake Britton that offers a good spot for a picnic and a swim.

CHAPTER FIVE

· · · · · · · · · ·

Hat Creek and Pit River Trails in the Vicinity of Highway 299

All the hikes described in this chapter take place on land owned by Pacific Gas and Electric (PG&E). Their present policy allows hikers access to this land, but the privilege could be revoked in the future. Any change in access policy will probably be evidenced by signs at or near the trailheads.

The Crystal Lake/Baum Lake trails (hike 37) and the four trails beginning at Hat Creek Park all travel near the cool environs of Hat Creek. This stream, which originates in the melting snow on the flanks of volcanic mountains in Lassen Park, provides some of the West's best trout fishing.

The Pit River to Lake Britton Trail (hike 42) and the Pit River Falls Trail (hike 43) border the Pit River, which begins on the western slopes of Modoc County's Warner Range. A few miles northeast of the falls are the

Exploring the shoreline of Crystal Lake

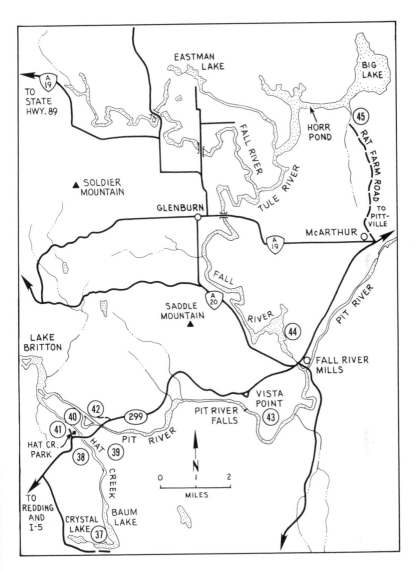

two lake hikes in the Fall River Valley: Fall River Lake (hike 44) and Big Lake/Horr Pond (hike 45).

Vegetation in the area consists of a mixture of foothill woodland and ponderosa-pine forest species. The Fall River Valley lakes, and to a lesser extent Lake Britton and Crystal and Baum lakes, host numerous types of water birds, especially during winter when thousands of migrating ducks and geese stop to feed and rest.

. . . .

37 CRYSTAL LAKE/BAUM LAKE

Jurisdiction and information: Recreation Department, PG&E, P.O. Box
277444, Sacramento, CA 95827. (800) 743-5000.
Length: Varies, up to 4.0 miles
Difficulty: Easy
Starting point: 3,000 feet
High point: 3,000 feet
Trail characteristics: Ranges from packed dirt to cinders to seasonally muddy
shoreline
Uses: Hiking
Season: Year-round
Facilities: Pit toilets at the parking area
Water: Bring your own
Map: USGS Burney

These two lakes provide year-round, easy hiking for the whole family. All
walking takes place near the lakes' shallow, placid waters, where you'll
find open views of the surrounding volcanic ridges and mountains.

The lakes often host migrating water birds. You'll see Canada geese,
several species of ducks, and many other types of aquatic birds. You can
also expect to see a few grazing cattle munching the green grasses growing
in flatter places near the water.

A wide variety of plants grows in this region. You'll see familiar
ponderosa pines and white and black oaks intermixed with western juniper,
a tree more common in desert areas to the east. Rabbit brush abounds in
open areas: its yellow flowers will delight you in late summer and early
fall. Cottonwoods and willows often line the lakeshore. Also, keep your
eyes open for poison oak.

Both Crystal and Baum lakes are primarily artificial, created by PG&E's
hydroelectric power operations. Since the two neighboring bodies of water
lie in the bottoms of flat valleys, the water is very shallow and thus not
suitable for swimming. However, the fishing is good. Numerous ambitious
anglers line the banks of both lakes and nearby Hat Creek, hoping to catch
trout.

Drive 2.0 miles east on Highway 299 past the intersection with Highway
89. Turn right where you see a sign for Crystal Lake State Fish Hatchery.
Follow this road 2.0 miles, then turn left and drive 1.0 mile. A sign will direct you to the parking area for Baum and Crystal lakes.

The narrow Crystal Lake sports views of Mount Shasta to the north and
Burney Mountain to the southwest. A faint trail hugs the shoreline along
the 2.0-mile circumference, but be prepared for muddy spots. It's less popular with fishermen, so you're more likely to find solitude. It also has more
waterfowl than Baum Lake.

To get to the lake, take the cinder-covered trail leaving from the west side of the parking lot. After crossing the dam separating the two lakes, follow the path along the north shore. You'll have no problems finding your way along the exposed shoreline.

Note the differences in vegetation between the north and south sides of the lake as you walk around it. Western juniper, squaw bush, and Oregon white oak predominate on the north side, whereas open forests of ponderosa pine and Oregon white oak inhabit the south side.

Baum Lake, formed by the damming of Hat Creek, runs north–south.

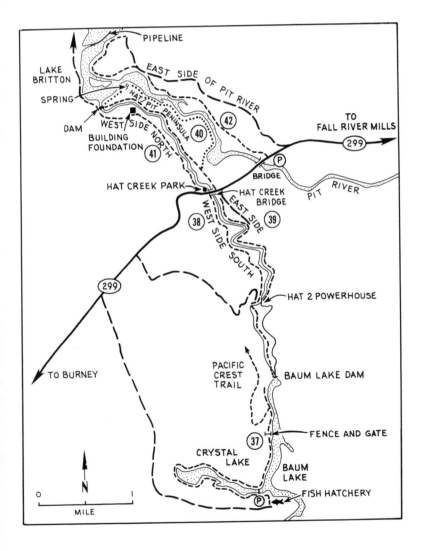

It's very popular with fishermen, but they all stay at the south end by the parking area.

The Pacific Crest Trail (PCT) goes along the west shore of Baum Lake. To reach it, take the short trail to Crystal Lake from the parking lot, then go right after you cross the dam. Head north, and the PCT will soon be apparent.

The trail parallels the shore and travels under ponderosa pine and black oak. You'll have good views of the lake itself, and also the ridge to the east, with its crown of crazily twisted digger pines.

After 0.5 mile you'll come to a fence with a barbed-wire gate. If it's closed, a double ladder will aid you in crossing. A few hundred yards later the PCT climbs southwest, then turns northwest 300 yards farther on its way to Burney Falls and Canada. Follow the PCT if you wish to extend your hike. It's well marked with white diamonds on trees, so you shouldn't lose your way.

From where the PCT heads uphill you can head down to the lakeshore and pick up a faint trail heading north towards the dam. It goes 0.25 mile through increasingly difficult terrain before disappearing into a dense thicket of brush.

38 WEST SIDE OF HAT CREEK SOUTH OF HIGHWAY 299

Jurisdiction and information: Recreation Department, PG&E, P.O. Box 277444, Sacramento, CA 95827. (800) 743-5000.
Length: 2.5 miles one way to Baum Lake Dam
Difficulty: Moderate
Starting point: 2,800 feet
High point: 3,000 feet
Trail characteristics: Ranges from good dirt road to narrow trails that are steep, slippery, wet, or near nonexistent
Uses: Hiking
Season: Year-round
Facilities: Pit toilets at Hat Creek Park
Water: Available from Hat Creek
Map: USGS Burney

This hike is for adventurous people willing and able to follow the faint trails that wind along the banks of Hat Creek and on up to Baum Lake. It offers many attractions: the soothing, placid waters of Hat Creek and the lush vegetation near its banks contrast with vistas of the valley and sur-

Yellow monkey flowers grow in damp areas near the banks of Hat Creek.

rounding mountains, and you'll gain understanding of how PG&E generates electricity.

From its intersection with Highway 89, follow Highway 299 east 4 miles, then turn left at Hat Creek Park.

To begin the hike, cross Highway 299 from Hat Creek Park and negotiate the fence by the bridge on the west side of Hat Creek. Here's a good rule of thumb for those worried about losing the trail: stay within 100 yards of the creek at all times on the way to the Hat 2 Powerhouse.

The trail is somewhat overgrown for the first few hundred yards, requiring careful attention on your part. It then opens up, allowing the first good views. One-half mile from Highway 299, the trail forks near a major westward bend in the creek. You can take either the high or low path: they rejoin a few hundred yards later. After reaching the reunion of the two trails near an old water ditch, follow a combination of old dirt roads and fisherman's trails to the parking lot by the powerhouse. (You can drive here by taking a road off Highway 299 about 1.0 mile west of Hat Creek Park.)

Once at the powerhouse, head uphill on the downstream side of the powerhouse complex, then hike up either side of the huge pipe. When you reach the top of the pipe, you'll see where water from the canal enters. This water comes from the dam at the southern end of Baum Lake, travels by canal to this spot, then has its gravitational potential energy changed to electrical power by rushing downhill through the pipe to turn turbines in the powerhouse. The turbines rotate giant magnets, which generate electricity.

To get to Baum Lake, the final destination of this hike, walk along either side of the canal. The west side provides easy traveling along a good dirt road. The bumpy east side, composed mostly of cinders, involves walking through occasional brush. From both sides you have exquisite views of Hat Creek Valley, Soldier Mountain, Saddle Mountain, and the other volcanic formations of the region.

At the Baum Lake Dam you'll see how Hat Creek's waters have been split: most enters the canal, but some continues down the natural course of the stream. A trail from the east side of the dam goes 0.25 mile down to the creek, and it's possible to hike cross-country along the east banks downstream to the area across from the powerhouse. From here you can take the trail along the east side back to Hat Creek Park (hike 39).

. . . .

39 EAST SIDE OF HAT CREEK SOUTH OF HIGHWAY 299

Jurisdiction and information: Recreation Department, PG&E, P.O. Box 277444, Sacramento, CA 95827. (800) 743-5000.
Length: Up to 1.4 miles one way
Difficulty: Easy
Starting point: 2,800 feet
High point: 2,850 feet
Trail characteristics: Ranges from good packed dirt to dusty diatomite to marshy areas near the creek
Uses: Hiking
Season: Year-round
Facilities: Pit toilets at Hat Creek Park
Water: Available from Hat Creek
Map: USGS Burney

This trail, especially popular with fishermen, offers almost continuous access to Hat Creek. There are actually two parallel trails: one is an old dirt road, the other is a footpath that runs closer to the banks of the creek.

Large ponderosa pine and Oregon white oak are the major tree species, and yellow-flowered rabbit brush covers much of the ground. However, the creek itself is the main attraction: its crystal-clear waters combine with a smooth reflective surface to mask the swift, underlying current.

From its intersection with Highway 89, follow Highway 299 east 4 miles, then turn left at Hat Creek Park. The trail begins on the southeast side of the Hat Creek Bridge. Initially you travel past cliffs of diatomite, the fossilized remains of tiny, silica-shelled lake dwellers that attest to the area's past as an ancient lake bed. The diatomite makes for a dusty trail, and in dry periods each step creates small, white dust clouds.

Both trails skirt some green meadows before the upper one ends at a parking area about 0.5 mile from the highway. From here the lower trail continues to follow the contours of the creek, passing through meadows much of the way. A few hundred yards past the parking area the trail becomes quite faint. You can hike all the way to an area across the creek from the Hat 2 Powerhouse (about 1.4 miles from the highway) but it involves getting your feet wet. No trails head up the east side of Hat Creek to Baum Lake, but it's possible to hike cross-country.

40 HAT CREEK/PIT RIVER PENINSULA

Jurisdiction and information: Recreation Department, PG&E, P.O. Box 277444, Sacramento, CA 95827. (800) 743-5000.
Length: 2.4–4.0 miles round-trip
Difficulty: Easy
Starting point: 2,800 feet
High point: 2,800 feet
Trail characteristics: Ranges from good dirt road to open cross-country; wear pants to keep brush from scratching your legs
Uses: Hiking
Season: Year-round
Facilities: Pit toilets at Hat Creek Park
Water: Available from Hat Creek
Map: USGS Burney

The land bordered by Hat Creek, the Pit River and Highway 299 provides some of the best hiking from Shasta County's Hat Creek Park. Faint, intermittent trails follow Hat Creek and the Pit River, and an old dirt road takes you to where the two streams intersect at Lake Britton. You can choose to hike nearly any place you wish: the open land makes cross-country hiking easy.

A hiker enjoys a view of Hat Creek.

From its intersection with Highway 89, follow Highway 299 east 4 miles, then turn left at Hat Creek Park. To begin hiking, go 50 feet east of the Hat Creek Bridge, then take the dirt road on your left. The road runs in a northwesterly direction, the same as the peninsula itself, and stays close to the banks of Hat Creek. It's about 1.2 miles from the highway to Lake Britton. As you progress you'll see Mount Shasta almost directly in front of you.

Black oak and Oregon white oak are the major tree species near water, with some ponderosa pine mixed in. Occasional buckbrush and Oregon white oak inhabit the central, open portion of the peninsula.

Water birds abound. At a minimum you can expect to see ducks and great blue herons, and possibly a bald eagle. Fishermen who hike out here can expect to fish in solitude, leaving their less energetic brethren behind.

Besides views and abundant wildlife, the peninsula has other attractions. Native Americans once lived here, and the old fruit trees of pioneer home-steaders who displaced them help instill a sense of history's movement.

Also, a secluded spring lies near the far end of the peninsula. Shaded by Oregon white oak, white alder, and a large ponderosa pine, it feeds a large,

1-foot-deep pool, from which a small creek flows down to Lake Britton. Birds love this peaceful spot, so don't be surprised if you scare up a great blue heron.

Consider making your trip a loop. Hike to Lake Britton on the road, with occasional forays down to Hat Creek, then follow the banks of the Pit River back towards Highway 299 until a fence edges you back to the dirt road.

. . . .

41 WEST SIDE OF HAT CREEK NORTH OF HIGHWAY 299

Jurisdiction and information: Recreation Department, PG&E, P.O. Box 277444, Sacramento, CA 95827. (800) 743-5000.
Length: 1.6 miles one way to Lake Britton
Difficulty: Moderate
Starting point: 2,800 feet
Low point: 2,750 feet
Trail characteristics: Ranges from good dirt road to faint, brush-intruded trail
Uses: Hiking
Season: Year-round
Facilities: Pit toilets at Hat Creek Park
Water: Available from Hat Creek
Map: USGS Burney

This hike, more enclosed by trees than other trails in the vicinity, only offers open views near the shore of Lake Britton. However, the trees themselves are quite pretty, especially in autumn when leaves turn color. Oregon white oak predominates, but you'll also see dogwood, ponderosa pine, and incense cedar.

From its intersection with Highway 89, follow Highway 299 east 4 miles, then turn left at Hat Creek Park. The trail begins near the creek at the northern edge of Hat Creek Park. You'll have to pick your own route to Lake Britton along the numerous roads and paths. If you stay within 100 yards of the creek you'll do fine.

A declining fruit orchard and the foundations of an old building, situated 1.0 mile from the park on a creek-side knoll, attest to the area's homesteader history. You'll also notice a dam at the mouth of Hat Creek. It prevents non-game fish from entering Hat Creek, a trophy trout stream.

A car parking area lies 200 yards past the dam.

If you wish to hike farther, there are several dirt roads to choose from, including one that follows some of Lake Britton's shoreline.

. . . .
42 PIT RIVER TO LAKE BRITTON TRAIL

Jurisdiction and information: Recreation Department, PG&E, P.O. Box
   277444, Sacramento, CA 95827. (800) 743-5000.
Length: 4.2-mile loop
Difficulty: Moderate
Starting point: 2,800 feet
High point: 2,900 feet
Trail characteristics: Ranges from good dirt road to faint, brushy trails
Uses: Hiking
Season: Year-round
Facilities: None
Water: Bring your own
Map: USGS Burney

This hike goes near the banks of the Pit River, then follows the shoreline of
Lake Britton before returning along dirt roads. It forms a loop that allows
both close-up views of the river and lake, and panoramic views of the surrounding mountains. The faint trails near the river and lake are a bit brushy
and occasionally require you to pick your own route.

From its intersection with Highway 89, follow Highway 299 east 5
miles. Park on the south side of the highway just past the second bridge (Pit
River Bridge).

To begin, cross to the north side of Highway 299 and follow the dirt
road. After curving left, head northwest (right) on the remains of an old
dirt road, now blocked by large rocks. As you parallel the Pit River, you
pass through mostly open grasslands. Oregon white oak grows down by the
river's banks, and a few western junipers and ponderosa pines dot the open
landscape away from the water.

About 1.4 miles from Highway 299, the Pit River abuts a cliff, forcing
you to climb up to a dirt road. Follow this road towards Lake Britton, turning left at a fork. The road grows ever fainter; just keep heading for the
lake's shore. (Once there you'll see a small, grassy island that you can visit
by wading through the lake's shallow waters.) Follow the shoreline for 0.5
mile as it curves in a northerly direction until you reach a pipeline that
crosses the lake. (Note: this area near the lake can be very muddy in winter
and spring.)

To complete the loop, go uphill to a dirt road. Follow this road in a generally southeast direction, bearing left at two successive forks over a 0.7-
mile stretch. Eventually you'll come to a good cinder road. Turn right and
go 1.2 miles back to Highway 299, where the road ends 200 yards east of
the parking area.

Pit River Falls lies at the bottom of a rock-walled canyon.

43 PIT RIVER FALLS TRAIL

Jurisdiction and information: Recreation Department, PG&E, P.O. Box
   277444, Sacramento, CA 95827. (800) 743-5000.
Length: 1.3 miles one way
Difficulty: Strenuous
Starting point: 3,350 feet
Low point: 2,950 feet
Trail characteristics: Steep and slippery in some areas, rocky in others
Uses: Hiking
Season: Year-round
Facilities: None
Water: Bring your own; water from the river probably isn't safe to drink
Map: USGS Jellico

Pit River Falls isn't easy to reach: you'll have to scramble down a slippery
dirt slope and deal with occasional brush in the trail (wear pants and boots).
Still, the wild beauty of the falls and the Pit River Canyon's 300-foot-high
walls make it all worthwhile.

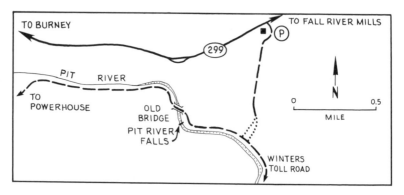

Take Highway 299 east from the intersection with Highway 89. About 0.5 mile east of the vista point, and 1.0 mile west of the town of Fall River Mills, is a large "Fall River Valley" sign. Turn south by the sign and park.

To begin the hike, follow the remnants of the old dirt road. It initially parallels the highway, then swings south. (You can drive 0.5 mile down this road if you're willing to punish your vehicle.) In this area, desert community plants intermingle with plants of the ponderosa pine and foothill woodland communities. Western juniper, rabbit brush, buckbrush, and occasional ponderosa and digger pines comprise the major plant species up here on the flat.

The dirt road ends 0.5 mile from the parking area at the edge of the Pit River Canyon. Two faint trails make their way to the bottom. It's best to take the one on the right as you face the canyon: it will spare you uncomfortable encounters with poison oak and squaw bush thickets. The trail is unmarked, so you'll have to use your best judgment in making your way.

Once at the bottom you'll find the old Winters Toll Road. This dirt road once connected the Fall River Valley with points west, and was in use as early as 1859. Turn right and walk past redbud, more squaw bush, and the occasional Oregon white oak.

As you walk along, look at the rocky sides of the Pit River Canyon, where you'll see layers from successive flows of hot liquid basalt. Holes caused by gas trapped in the quickly cooled molten rock riddle the basalt talus that's fallen from the cliffs.

After walking 0.5 mile along the Winters Toll Road you'll come to the falls. The roaring waters tumble more than 30 feet into turbulent pools, sending up a spray of fine mist. You can easily get down next to the falls for close observation and perhaps a picnic. An area of relatively slow-moving water 100 feet below the falls makes an excellent swimming spot.

Just downstream of the falls you'll see remnants of the old iron bridge that linked the Winters Toll Road with its continuation on the other side. Much of the flooring of the bridge is missing, and it's too dangerous to cross.

. . . .

44   FALL RIVER LAKE

Jurisdiction and information: Recreation Department, PG&E, P.O. Box
   277444, Sacramento, CA 95827. (800) 743-5000.
Length: Variable; up to 4.0 miles total
Difficulty: Easy
Starting point: 3,300 feet
High point: 3,300 feet
Trail characteristics: Flat dirt roads; easy walking
Uses: Hiking, biking
Season: Year-round
Facilities: None
Water: Bring your own
Map: USGS Fall River Mills

The east side of Fall River Lake is a great place to watch the beautiful sun-
sets that grace the Fall River Valley. Soldier Mountain and Saddle Mountain frame the contrasting shades of pink and purple, and the whole picture
is reflected in the lake's waters as ducks and other water birds engage in
their final activities of the day. However, this area rates a visit at any hour.

There are several dirt roads on the east side of the lake for you to choose
from. You'll probably want to hike on the roads closest to the shore, for
these have the best views of the lake and the mountains ringing the valley.
The open terrain is relatively flat, with western juniper and ponderosa pine
interspersed between rabbit brush and buckbrush. Willows grow near the
lakeshore, where they find the large quantities of water they require.

Go to the town of Fall River Mills, located 65 miles east of Redding on

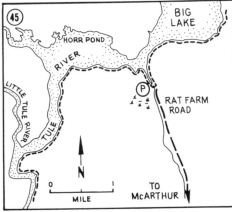

Highway 299. Turn north on Third Street, then east (right) on Burney Street. The parking area is located just east of Fall River Elementary School.

To begin hiking, go through the gate on the north side of the parking area, then head northwest on the dirt road toward the lake. You can hike 1.5 miles to an old fruit orchard to the north, and also go down by the dam on the south side of the lake.

Fall River Lake is quite popular with boaters and fishermen, who usually access the lake from the west side by turning north on Long Street. The relatively large numbers of vehicles and people make this side less attractive for hikers, but still worthwhile. You can hike the roads or along the shoreline.

. . . .

45 BIG LAKE/HORR POND

Jurisdiction and information: Recreation Department, PG&E, P.O. Box 277444, Sacramento, CA 95827. (800) 743-5000.
Length: Up to 4.0 miles one way
Difficulty: Easy to moderate
Starting point: 3,300 feet
High point: 3,300 feet
Trail characteristics: All hiking is on levees; trails are mostly due to the large number of cattle roaming the area—watch where you step; levees are composed of fine material, and can be slippery in winter and spring
Uses: Hiking
Season: Year-round
Facilities: Pit toilets at the parking area
Water: Bring your own
Map: USGS Fall River Mills

There are two good reasons for visiting this area. First: the birds. The open fields bordering the two interconnected lakes make prime hunting grounds for hawks. And if you're lucky, you might also spot a great horned owl perched in a tree.

However, the most conspicuous birds are the water birds, which you'll see in abundance. Many different species live here, either seasonally or permanently. Huge white pelicans force their heavy bodies into the air, then make their way to another resting spot with an awkward gracefulness. Great blue herons abound: you should surprise several into flight during your hike. In addition, there's the usual assortment of pintail and mallard ducks, Canada geese, mergansers, and other aquatic birds. Duck hunters love this area, so you might want to avoid it during the fall hunting season.

The other main attraction is the 360-degree panoramic view. The glaciered slopes of Mount Shasta dominate the north, Mount Burney and the Thousand Lakes Wilderness's Crater and Magee peaks the southwest, and Mount Lassen and Prospect Peak the south. All these peaks, and the nearer mountains which ring the Fall River Valley, owe their existence to volcanic activity.

Vulcanism is also indirectly responsible for the formation of both Tule and Fall rivers, and Big Lake and Horr Pond. These arise from nearby springs, the waters of which originate in the area of Tule Lake, 60 miles to the north. This water percolates underground through porous volcanic rock to emerge here.

Take Highway 299 east of Redding 70 miles to the town of McArthur. Turn north (left) on Main Street, and follow it past the fairgrounds. It quickly becomes a dirt road that can be impassable after heavy rains. Bear right 0.5 mile from the highway and pass through a green gate, which you must open and close. Continue north another 3.0 miles to the parking area.

There are two directions in which you can hike. The first heads along the southeastern shore of Big Lake. After a little more than 1.0 mile you'll reach the water's eastern end, where the trail becomes a road, which quickly heads into private property.

The second direction initially takes you west along the southern shore of Horr Pond for the first 1.5 miles, then heads southwest for 2.5 miles through farm and ranch country along the banks of the Tule River. Purple star thistle and other weeds can intrude both trails, especially in summer. Prepare for numerous encounters with cattle, which are generally very gracious about yielding the right-of-way. Also, there's no shade, so protect yourself from the sun. The extremely shallow water means there's little opportunity for swimming.

CHAPTER SIX

· · · · · · · · · ·

Redding/Anderson/Red Bluff Vicinity

The Sacramento River begins high in the mountains of Northern California and gathers the waters of other rivers and creeks as it courses southward to the San Francisco Bay. Five of this chapter's hikes border this mighty stream. The Sacramento River Trail (hike 46), Turtle Bay Trails (hike 47), the Olney Creek/ Cascade Community Park Trails (hike 48), the Anderson River Park Trail (hike 49), and the Paynes Creek/Sacramento River Area (hike 50) all take you by the lush, green riparian plant species lining the river's banks. Dozens of different bird species from this and surrounding habitats make these hikes a bird-watcher's dream.

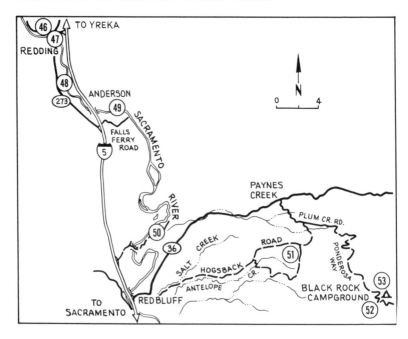

The surrounding foothills, which often border the river itself, rise to meet the mighty Klamath and Cascade mountains that ring the upper Sacramento Valley. Four hikes allow you to explore these oak-and-pine-covered slopes: the Paynes Creek/Sacramento River Area (hike 50), the Tehama Wildlife Area (hike 51), and the lower and upper Mill Creek trails (hikes 52 and 53). As you hike, look for dark basaltic rock lining the rims of canyons and lying scattered on the ground. This rock is the remains of extensive lava flows that covered the area tens of millions of years ago.

. . . .

46 SACRAMENTO RIVER TRAIL

Jurisdiction and information: City of Redding Recreation and Parks Department, P.O. Box 496071, Redding, CA 96049. (916) 225-4095.
Length: 5.5-mile loop, plus a 1.7-mile extension
Difficulty: Easy to moderate
Starting point: 550 feet
High point: 600 feet
Trail characteristics: Trail is 6 feet wide, paved, and almost entirely flat
Uses: Hiking, biking, horseback riding
Season: Year-round
Facilities: Pit toilets along the trail 400 yards west of the south trailhead and 250 yards southeast of the footbridge on the north side. Caldwell Park has modern bathrooms, playgrounds, and picnic tables
Water: Available from drinking fountains at the south trailhead, the end of Harlan Drive, and Caldwell Park
Map: USGS Redding

The popular Sacramento River Trail is a great place to see the citizens of the Redding area in a relaxed state. Whether walking, jogging, cycling, or roller-skating, everybody is friendly, greeting one another with smiles and hellos. If you find the trail itself too crowded, take any of the numerous dirt paths and roads down along the banks of both sides of the river, or hike on the gravel-covered railroad bed just uphill from the trail on the river's south side.

The trail offers a mix of human and natural history, succinctly explained by numerous interpretive signs located along the trail. For example, you'll learn about gold mining techniques, interesting aspects of beaver life, and the local history of the Central Pacific Railroad.

In Redding, take the Highway 299 West exit off I-5. Turn right onto Market Street, then left onto Riverside Drive. The large south trailhead parking lot is at the bottom of the hill. There are three other trail access points from the river's north side. To reach the first, continue across the river from the south trailhead parking lot, then turn left into the parking lot by the Senior Citizen's Center. To reach the second, continue across the river and turn left on Quartz Hill Road. Turn left again on Harlan Drive and follow it to the end. To reach the third, turn left off Harlan Drive onto Lake Redding Drive, where you'll find a sign for the trail. Neither the second nor third access point has much parking.

Since the vast majority of hikers begin at the south trailhead, the trail is described from this point. The trail's first 1.5 miles closely follow the banks of the river, passing through typical riparian vegetation. Cottonwood trees, most numerous near the trailhead, tower high above. Two nonnative species, ailanthus and black locust, are well represented, as are white alders near the river's edge. Willows, redbud, and blackberries comprise the most common understory plants, and wild grapevines grow over and through everything.

One and a half miles from the trailhead, the trail moves away from the river to follow the track bed of the old Central Pacific Railroad in the direction of distant Shasta Bally. A dry, rocky stretch of land lies between the trail and the river; a network of roads makes it easy to explore.

The bridge spanning the river, built in 1990, lies 2.5 miles from the trailhead. Two nearby picnic tables make a great place to rest and eat lunch. A dirt road continues 0.5 mile north along the river to Keswick Dam, ending at Keswick Dam Road. One hundred yards north of the bridge, and just down from the dirt road, an interpretive sign describes Waugh's Ferry, which transported gold miners across the river between 1853 and 1883.

The trail on the north side differs from that on the south side in three ways. First, it climbs up and down the hillsides, giving the legs a change from level walking. Second, it offers open views of Shasta Bally and South Fork to the west, Mount Lassen and the Cascades to the east, and the mansions of Redding's well-to-do standing shoulder to shoulder atop the cliff to the south. Third, it travels through vegetation very different from the riparian species found on the river's south side. The south-facing hills are

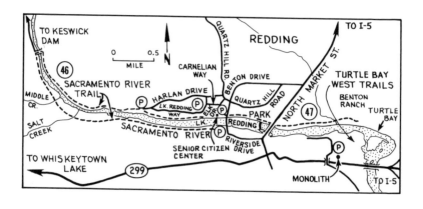

Wild grape leaves; wild grape vines often climb trees near water.

exposed to more sunlight and receive little or no moisture from the river. Thus the plants found on these hillsides are typical foothill woodland species: blue oak, interior live oak, whiteleaf manzanita, greenleaf manzanita, buckbrush, toyon, and yerba santa.

The trail winds 1.4 miles from the footbridge past several interpretive signs before reaching a drinking fountain at the end of Harlan Road. Follow Harlan Road for 200 yards, then turn right onto the paved path. The trail skirts backyards for 0.8 mile, passing by some huge valley oaks and a mixture of riparian and foothill vegetation, then ends at the trail access point on Lake Redding Drive.

To walk the last 0.5 mile back to the south trailhead, turn right on Carnelian Way, cross Elk Drive, then pass through the parking lot by the Senior Citizen's Center to Benton Drive. A short walk across the Deistlehorst Bridge will bring you back to your starting point.

The 1.7-mile-long extension of the Sacramento River Trail begins under Deistlehorst Bridge. The first 0.8 mile goes through Caldwell Park, where large valley oaks, cottonwood trees, California sycamores, and many other trees and shrubs provide ample shade and verdant scenery.

After passing under the Market Street bridge, the path quickly enters the Redding Arboretum. An interpretive nature brochure helps guide you through the three-mile system of trails. Look for riparian plant species, such as cottonwood and willow, near the river and Sulfur Creek. The upland areas host blue oak, whiteleaf and greenleaf manzanita, and buckbrush.

The Sacramento River Trail system may be expanded in the future. Tentative plans call for extending the trail on the north side past Keswick Dam all the way to Shasta Dam. Also, a bridge may be built across the river from Benton Ranch to Turtle Bay (hike 47).

The "monolith" once was the departure point for Turtle Bay gravel bound for the Shasta Dam construction site.

47 TURTLE BAY TRAILS

Jurisdiction and information: City of Redding Recreation and Parks Department, P.O. Box 496071, Redding, CA 96049. (916) 225-4095.
Length: Variable, up to 2.0 miles
Difficulty: Easy
Starting point: 550 feet
High point: 550 feet
Trail characteristics: Ranges from wide gravel roads to packed dirt paths
Uses: Hiking, mountainbiking
Season: Year-round
Facilities: Bathrooms by the boat-launching ramp west of the parking lot
Water: Available from drinking fountains near the bandstand
Map: USGS Redding

Turtle Bay, a quiet sanctuary nestled within Redding, offers a welcome respite from the hustle and bustle of the growing city. It's also an area rich in both human and natural history, and contains a multitude of interconnecting trails and roads which allow thorough exploration. This entry doesn't specifically describe the trails and roads, but you'll quickly discover your own favorite routes.

Take the Park Marina Drive/Auditorium Drive exit off Highway 299 in Redding, 0.5 mile west of I-5. Head north towards the Civic Auditorium, then take the first right. Park in the lot on your left.

The present topography and appearance of Turtle Bay is intimately linked with the construction of Shasta Dam in the late 1930s and 1940s. The most striking relic of this time is the edifice known as "the monolith," a major Redding landmark. An imposing structure, the monolith was used to lift excavated river gravel onto conveyor belts, which then transported the gravel 9 miles north to the dam site, where it was used to make concrete to fill the dam. A few hundred yards north of the monolith, near the bandstand, is one of the cement structures that supported the conveyor belt.

The construction of Shasta Dam prevented the yearly floods of land along the river and allowed many different species of plants that couldn't tolerate flooding to grow. Thus a diversity of ecosystems flourishes within the small confines of the park.

Several ponds, which receive their water from underground river seepage, teem with a multitude of aquatic animals and plants. Sit quietly among the bordering cattails and grasses and allow shy animals such as turtles, bullfrogs, and muskrats to show themselves.

The Sacramento River harbors many species of fish, and you'll see numerous hopeful anglers on the banks or wading in the water. Many species of aquatic birds, such as herons, egrets, Canada geese, and several types of ducks, grace the waters of the river and ponds. Other animals you may see are beaver, muskrat, skunks, raccoons, squirrels, and wild house cats.

The diversity of plant species more than matches the diversity of animals. Higher, drier areas away from the water have typical foothill species such as digger pine, interior live oak, and whiteleaf and greenleaf manzanita.

Near the ponds and the river's banks you'll see species typical of wet places in Northern California: cottonwood, white alder, ailanthus, and black locust. Numerous shrubs grow, with willow and blackberries being the most prominent.

Future plans for Turtle Bay include developing some of the trails and possibly constructing a bridge across the river to the Sacramento River Trail (hike 46).

· ·

48 OLNEY CREEK/CASCADE COMMUNITY PARK TRAILS

Jurisdiction and information: City of Redding Recreation and Parks Department, P.O. Box 496071, Redding, CA 96049. (916) 225-4095.
Length: 1.5 miles of trails
Difficulty: Easy
Starting point: 525 feet
High point: 525 feet
Trail characteristics: Easy walking on a paved path and a wide dirt trail
Uses: Hiking, mountainbiking
Season: Year-round
Facilities: Picnic tables, playground
Water: Available from a fountain at Cascade Community Park
Map: USGS Redding

A combination of beauty, accessibility, and wide range of recreational options makes this trail system a favorite destination for locals. Cascade Park has basketball courts, a playground, and green lawns, and is a good place for a picnic. Olney Creek and the Sacramento River offer havens of riparian solitude, away from the sights and sounds of the surrounding suburbs.

From Highway 273 in south Redding, head east on Girvan Road 0.6 mile to Cascade Community Park.

A 0.5-mile-long concrete path encircles the park. About halfway around, a dirt path goes down to the confluence of Olney Creek and the Sacramento River. This secluded spot is a favorite with great blue herons and other water birds. A dirt road running parallel to the main loop trail on the east side allows access to lush river views in several places.

Cattails often grow in damp soils near streams like Olney Creek.

The 0.8-mile-long Olney Creek Trail begins on the opposite side of Girvan Road from Cascade Community Park, and runs along the creek's east bank. Olney Creek, a year-round stream, originates in the hills west of Redding. Although it flows through semi-urban areas, it attracts a surprising amount of wildlife, including deer, beaver, and trout. Giant valley oaks guard the creek's banks and overshadow willows and blackberry vines. A

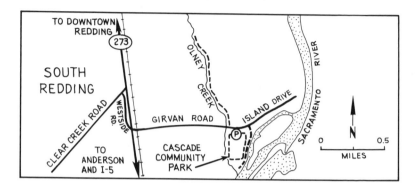

small pond located 0.25 mile from Girvan Road shelters catfish, turtles, and giant bullfrogs. In spring, trailside meadows erupt in a multicolored carpet of flowers; most are native, but many exotic species have migrated from nearby homes.

49 ANDERSON RIVER PARK TRAIL

Jurisdiction and information: City of Anderson Parks and Recreation Department, 1887 Howard Street, Anderson, CA 96007. (916) 378-6656.
Length: 0.7-mile, paved loop trail, plus 1.5 miles of additional trails and dirt roads
Difficulty: Easy
Starting point: 500 feet
High point: 500 feet
Trail characteristics: Ranges from pavement to packed dirt
Uses: Hiking, biking. Horses are allowed, but must stay off the loop trail's pavement
Season: Year-round
Hours open: Sunrise–11:00 P.M.
Facilities: Playgrounds, picnic tables; bathrooms are located at the picnic area just north of the parking area
Water: Available from a drinking fountain by the bathrooms
Map: USGS Anderson

The Anderson River Park Trail compares favorably with the Sacramento River Trail (hike 46) found just north in the town of Redding. While Redding's trail is longer and has numerous interpretive signs, it's also heavily used. In pleasant contrast, Anderson's trail is less crowded, and numerous dirt trails and roads lead to quiet, secluded spots nestled underneath the shade of valley oaks and giant cottonwood trees. Several shallow ponds bordering the trail sport a variety of wetland plants and provide excellent habitat for egrets, ducks, geese, and other water birds.

If heading north on I-5, take the Central Anderson/Lassen Park exit. Turn right onto Balls Ferry Road, then left onto Stingy Lane, then right onto Rupert Road. If heading south on I-5, take the Anderson exit. Turn left onto North Street, then right onto Stingy Lane, then left onto Rupert Road. Rupert Road leads to the park. Follow the main road through the park, then turn left onto a dirt road at a small sign saying "KC Grove." Park by the children's playground.

To hike the paved loop trail, head to the right from the playground towards a wooden bridge. Turn left at a fork, then take the bridge over the pond. You'll shortly encounter another fork: stay left for the main trail.

As you continue, you'll notice several dirt paths leading east through willows and ailanthus trees. By following these interconnected trails, you'll come to the river near an area of small rapids. A gravel bar runs parallel to the river here, and has a wide variety of multicolored, water-

A young family crosses a bridge between two ponds at Anderson River Park.

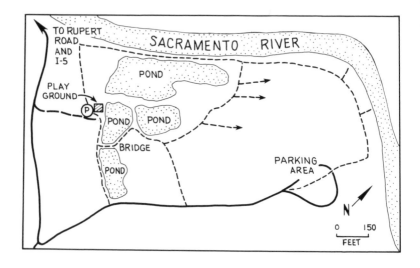

smoothed rocks that make good skipping stones.

The loop trail eventually reaches the river's edge, where a bench invites you to sit and view the water and the vegetation on the river's far side. From here, the route travels atop a levee, with the river on the right and ponds on the left. Finally, the trail borders a picnic area and returns to the playground.

50 PAYNES CREEK/SACRAMENTO RIVER AREA

Jurisdiction and information: Bureau of Land Management, 355 Hemsted, Redding, CA 96002. (916) 224-2100.
Length: Variable, up to 10.0 miles
Difficulty: Easy to moderate, depending on route chosen
Starting point: 350 feet
High point: Variable, up to 750 feet
Trail characteristics: Varies from flat dirt road to faint, brushy river trails to cross-country
Uses: Hiking, mountainbiking, horseback riding
Season: Year-round
Facilities: None
Water: None, bring your own
Map: USGS Tuscan Butte

Hiking this area requires initiative and a willingness to explore. As this book goes to press, there are no established trails, though tentative plans call for such development in the future. Sections of rough trail exist in some areas, and several dirt roads provide easy hiking. However, cross-country hiking is necessary to reach many of the prettier areas. You can wander where you like: boundaries are generally marked by Bureau of Land Management (BLM) signs. Winter and spring offer the best hiking: green grass and wildflowers are better than the heat and stickers of summer and fall. Be sure to keep track of direction: it's easy to get lost out here, especially on cloudy days. Use Table Mountain on the west side of the river as a marker.

Take the Jellys Ferry Road exit off I-5 4 miles north of Red Bluff. Head east 2.6 miles, then bear right onto Bend Ferry Road. Follow the twists and turns of this paved road for 2.4 miles to the signed beginning of BLM land. From now on you'll be driving on a bumpy dirt road. A covered signboard on the left has a good map of the area. (You can do a short walk around the pond just west of this sign, and also follow a path down to the river.) From the signboard continue 0.7 mile to a fork below some powerlines: bear right. Bear left 0.4 mile later at a road fork, and continue 0.7 mile to the wide parking area at the road's end.

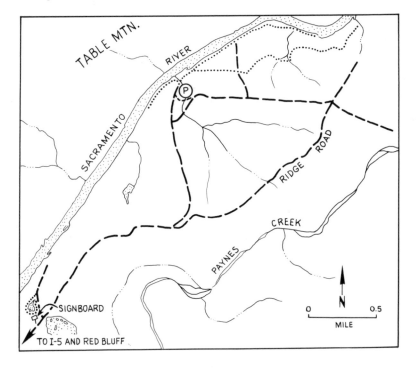

In places, massive valley oaks line the banks of the Sacramento River.

There are two main hiking options from the main parking area. For the first option, take the small trail that leaves from the east side. It quickly crosses a seasonal creek, then meets a dirt road. This dirt road heads northeast, and from it you can explore the hills and valleys that stretch in all directions, either cross-country or by taking any of the several intersecting roads and paths. Only blue oak and occasional buckbrush dot these hills, leaving you ample room to maneuver. From higher ridges the magnificent mountains of Northern California present a visual delight.

The second hiking option focuses on the Sacramento River, which slows to a placid crawl in this region. Fish leap from the surface under the hungry watch of great blue herons, and river otters congenially cavort with one another, both on the banks and in the water. Winter brings flocks of majestic

Canada and snow geese, which share this area with many other water birds. Huge cottonwoods, sycamores, and valley oaks line the river's banks, shading willows and other riparian vegetation.

A dirt road on the west side of the parking lot goes downhill to the river. From here you have two choices. You can hike upstream (northeast) near the river by following an intermittent trail that often disappears into yellow star thistle thickets.

The second option, hiking in the upstream (northeast) direction along the hills' open ridge, offers great views. You'll see the river, Table Mountain on the river's far side, and the surrounding hills and mountains. It is also much easier walking.

Combining the two main hiking options presents little difficulty, and will be preferred by those who like walking longer distances. As you hike northeast, either along the river or in the hills, you'll encounter Cenozoic volcanic rocks, which litter the ground and occasionally form bizarre columns. This is the only known place where Cascade lava flows reached the Sacramento River.

51 TEHAMA WILDLIFE AREA

Jurisdiction and information: California Fish and Game Department, 601 Locust Street, Redding, CA 96001. (916) 225-2300.
Length: Varies
Difficulty: Easy to moderate
Starting point: Variable, averages 2,100 feet
High point: Variable, maximum of 3,300 feet
Trail characteristics: No official trails; hikers can walk on old dirt roads or make their way cross-country through terrain that varies from open grassland to thick brush; some areas are almost totally covered with volcanic rocks
Uses: Hiking, mountainbiking, horseback riding
Season: Year-round, but nicest in winter and spring. The area south of Hogsback Road is closed from December 1 through April 7
Facilities: None
Water: Available from Antelope Creek and seasonal creeks, but it's best to bring your own
Maps: USGS Red Bluff, USGS Panther Spring, and USGS Manton

The Tehama Wildlife Area's 44,601 acres of land beckon the adventurous hiker. There are no established trails here; you'll have to pick your own routes according to what tickles your fancy. Try to find old dirt roads that take off from the main dirt road, or open grassland. Actually, the two main dirt roads, Hogsback and Ishi, offer the easiest hiking, and there is very little traffic to disturb you. A cautionary note: it's easy to get lost when hiking cross-country, so bring a compass, look for familiar landmarks, and make sure you keep your bearings straight.

Two different plant communities intermingle here. Foothill woodland species such as digger pine and blue oak, which flourish at lower elevations, grow in abundance. Ponderosa pine and black oak, which are more prevalent at higher elevations, have also established themselves. Be pre-

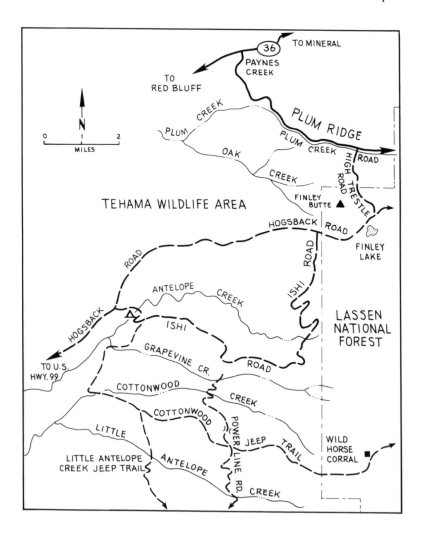

pared for buckbrush and occasional thick mats of yellow star thistle.

From I-5, take the Highway 99 exit in Red Bluff, then head east to Highway 36. Drive 20 miles up Highway 36 to the town of Paynes Creek. Turn right on Paynes Creek Road, then right again on Plum Creek Road. Follow Plum Creek Road 5.0 miles until you see a yellow "icy" sign on the right. Turn right onto the dirt road just before this sign. Once on the dirt road you'll see a sign for Finley Lake and Antelope Creek.

After leaving the paved Plum Creek Road, you'll be driving on dirt roads of varying though tolerable quality the rest of the way. Nearly 2.5 miles after leaving Plum Creek Road, turn right onto the unsigned Hogsback Road. (Left leads into Lassen National Forest land, where you can also hike.)

Hogsback Road is the main route in the Tehama Wildlife Area, and goes all the way down to Highway 99 in Red Bluff. As you drive west, begin looking for hiking places.

Some of the best hiking requires driving down the unmarked Ishi Road, which leaves on the left 1.8 miles after you join Hogsback. It takes you to Antelope Creek, where you'll find steep volcanic rock walls lining the creek's canyon. This area south of Hogsback Road serves as winter range for deer, and is off limits from December 1 through April 7. Ishi Road eventually rejoins Hogsback Road several miles after crossing Antelope Creek (which can be very dangerous for vehicles during periods of high water flow) but the last 0.5 mile requires 4-wheel drive.

52 LOWER MILL CREEK TRAIL

Jurisdiction and information: Almanor Ranger District, Lassen National Forest, P.O. Box 767, Chester, CA 96020. (916) 258-2141.
Length: 4.7 miles one way to the intersection with the Rancheria Trail
Difficulty: Moderate
Starting point: 2,100 feet
Low point: 1,700 feet
Trail characteristics: A few mucky spots and areas where the trail is a bit faint, but generally easy walking
Uses: Hiking, horseback riding
Season: April through November. Or anytime you think you can navigate the dirt roads, which are very muddy in winter
Facilities: Pit toilets at Black Rock Campground by the trailhead
Water: Available from Mill Creek and its numerous tributary springs and creeks
Maps: USGS Panther Spring and USGS Butte Meadows

The Ishi Wilderness, part of the Lassen National Forest, lies in the rugged foothills of the Cascades. The region's volcanic activity is clearly evidenced by the stark basaltic cliffs lining the canyons, and in the many strangely shaped lava formations. Spring-fed streams flow abundantly through the canyons they have carved in their westerly rush to join the Sacramento River. This constant supply of cool water contrasts dramatically with the hot temperatures that prevail in this low-elevation area during summer.

The wilderness area is named after the last surviving Yahi Native American, a man known as Ishi. The Yahi lived in the rugged canyons of the Ishi Wilderness and surrounding area for thousands of years. They survived in the mild climate by hunting deer and other animals, fishing for salmon, and eating a variety of edible plants.

Along with many other tribes in California, the Yahi were systematically exterminated by the white settlers who streamed west during the middle of the nineteenth century. Beginning in 1870, Ishi and the last few remaining members of the Yahi managed to hide out in the upper reaches of the Mill Creek and Deer Creek canyons. In 1911, Ishi, the last living member of the Yahi, was discovered by whites and taken to San Francisco, where he spent much of his remaining years relating the Yahi's way of life to anthropologists.

As you hike through this wilderness area, you will often be on trails made by the Yahi. No doubt some of the flat meadows near the creek were used as campsites. Please remember that all archaeological sites and historical remains should not be disturbed.

The Lower Mill Creek Trail winds up and down the north side of Mill Creek Canyon, passing by numerous springs and several creeks. Sheer volcanic rock cliffs tower high above, and there are spectacular views of the canyon walls and cool rushing waters of Mill Creek. Mill Creek maintains a high water flow year-round, and several side trails from the main trail lead to swimming areas.

Take Highway 36 from Red Bluff 20 miles to the town of Paynes Creek.

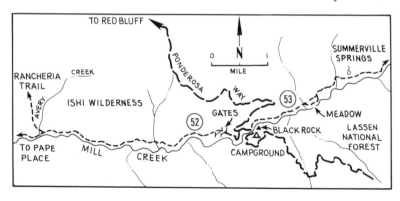

The imposing face of Black Rock looks down on the boulder-strewn waters of Mill Creek.

Turn right onto Paynes Creek Road, then right again 0.3 mile farther onto Plum Creek Road. Follow this paved road for 8.0 miles, then turn right onto Ponderosa Way, where signs will direct you towards Black Rock. Ponderosa Way, composed of dirt and some gravel, is the main drag for this section of the Lassen National Forest. At all intersections follow the signs for Black Rock and/or Mill Creek, which will always direct you to the best maintained road. Three and a half miles after turning onto Ponderosa Way you must drive through Antelope Creek where it overflows a cement culvert. This could be difficult for some vehicles during periods of high water flow. Black Rock Campground (four campsites), where the trailhead is located, is 20 miles from the intersection of Ponderosa Way and Plum Creek Road. The last 5.0 miles are narrow and a bit rough.

The signed trail begins from the west side of Black Rock Campground, farthest away from Ponderosa Way. After climbing a bit, you'll join a dirt road for 400 yards until reaching the locked gate of a private ranch. A sign directs you through another gate on the right. For the next few hundred yards you'll walk through muddy, spring-fed meadows amid numerous cattle.

Once the ranch and muck are left behind, it's relatively smooth sailing. The trail gently rises and falls through open woodlands of interior live, blue, and black oak. The dominant pine tree is the digger, but occasional stands of majestic ponderosa occupy the flats near Mill Creek, with some incense cedar mixed in. Canyon live oaks and California laurel congregate in moist shaded areas, and are often festooned with hanging vines of wild grape.

Most of the rock around you is volcanic. However, you'll occasionally see some exposed sedimentary rock. Also, be sure to observe the south rim of the canyon: you should see areas burned in a 1990 fire.

About 3 miles from the trailhead you'll come to more meadows, most likely populated by cows. The trail continues, crossing Avery Creek, and finally intersecting the signed Rancheria Trail. This faint, steep trail heads north to the boundary of Ishi Wilderness. Those wishing to extend their hike can climb up this trail or continue west another 2.0 miles to Pape Place along the main trail.

. . . .
53 UPPER MILL CREEK TRAIL

Jurisdiction and information: Almanor Ranger District, Lassen National Forest, P.O. Box 767, Chester, CA 96020. (916) 258-2141.
Length: Up to 13.0 miles one way
Difficulty: Moderate
Starting point: 2,100 feet
High point: 2,500 feet 3.0 miles from the trailhead
Trail characteristics: Good trail; mucky in some wet areas
Uses: Hiking, horseback riding
Season: April to November. Or anytime, if you're willing to risk the muddy roads in winter
Facilities: Pit toilets at Black Rock Campground
Water: Available from Mill Creek, springs, and small creeks
Map: USGS Butte Meadows

The Upper Mill Creek Trail offers similar topography and vegetation as Lower Mill Creek Trail. The trail goes for 13 miles, so you can hike as far as you want, then turn back. Although not part of the official Ishi Wilderness, this trail also passes through territory of the Yahi Indians.

As with the lower trail, several side trails go down to Mill Creek. Swimming holes, while not abundant, can be found by those who seek them out.

Take Highway 36 from Red Bluff 20 miles to the town of Paynes Creek. Turn right onto Paynes Creek Road, then right again 0.3 mile farther onto Plum Creek Road. Follow this paved road for 8.0 miles, then turn right onto Ponderosa Way, where signs will direct you towards Black Rock. Ponderosa Way, composed of dirt and some gravel, is the main drag for this section of the Lassen National Forest. At all intersections follow the signs for Black Rock and/or Mill Creek, which will always direct you to the best maintained road. Three and a half miles after turning onto Ponderosa Way you must drive through Antelope Creek where it overflows a cement culvert. This could be difficult for some vehicles during periods of high water flow. Black Rock Campground (four campsites), where the trailhead is located, is 20 miles from the intersection of Ponderosa Way and Plum Creek Road. The last 5.0 miles are narrow and a bit rough.

The trail begins from Ponderosa Way about 150 feet north of the turnoff to Black Rock Campground. After 100 yards a side trail leads to an overlook with spectacular views of Black Rock and the madly rushing waters of Mill Creek.

After 1.0 mile of easy hiking, the trail forks just past a small creek. You can choose either way, but the right-hand fork is best. It goes through the lower reaches of a lush meadow, where you'll find remnants of an old fruit orchard and easy access to the creek. At the east end of the meadow is a reasonably good swimming hole. Both options involve crossing through squishy mud and negotiating around a few blackberry vines. One hundred yards past the end of the meadow the two forks rejoin.

One-half mile past the meadow the trail crosses a cool, shaded creek, then climbs. After contouring the mountainside for 0.25 mile, it reaches Summerville Springs, an area of lush, water-fed greenery stretching 100 yards across an otherwise dry landscape. Several tree species grow here, but the most unusual is the California nutmeg. This rare tree has sharp, dark blue-green needles and may have brown nuts. However, it does not produce the tastebud titillater like that of its relative from the Spice Islands. One-half mile past Summerville Springs lies a flat near the creek with several large ponderosa pines, including some dead snags. The trail continues east up the creek for another 10 miles, offering scenery similar to that previously encountered.

CHAPTER SEVEN

The Yolla Bollys and the Coast Range

The mountains bordering the Sacramento Valley's west side rise steeply from the foothills to heights as great as 8,092 feet, beckoning the adventurous to explore their secluded, windswept peaks. This chapter includes this rugged area's three most spectacular hikes: the North Yolla Bolly trails (hike 54), which take you to two lakes and to the tops of two peaks; the Ides Cove Loop Trail (hike 55), which takes you to two lakes and to the top of Mount Linn, the highest peak in the Yolla Bollys; and the Snow Moun-

North Yolla Bolly Mountain looms above Pettijohn Meadows on the way to Black Rock Lake (hike 54).

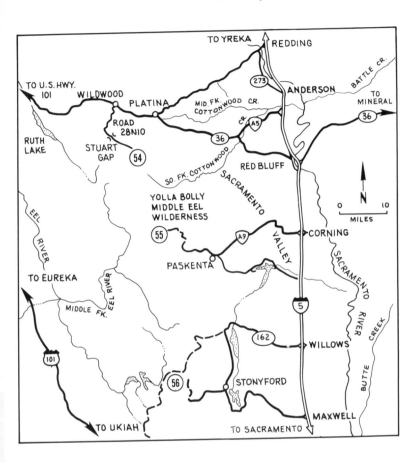

tain Trail (hike 56), which takes you to the multicolored twin summits of
Snow Mountain.

All three hikes begin in the red-fir forest plant community, where red fir
and Jeffrey pine are the most numerous trees. However, on the mountain
summits you'll find the relatively rare foxtail pine, part of the higher subal-
pine plant community.

Most rocks you'll see in the Yolla Bollys are metamorphic. Especially
noticeable are Graywacke sandstone along the Ides Cove Loop Trail (hike
55) and chert and greenstone along the Snow Mountain Trail (hike 56).

The elevation and remoteness of these three hikes require that you be
prepared: take extra clothing and a tarp or poncho in case a sudden storm
strikes, and take note of the hiking season: June through October. Also,
hike with friends to ensure that you could help each other if an emergency
were to arise.

54 NORTH YOLLA BOLLY TRAILS

Jurisdiction and information: Yolla Bolly Ranger District, Shasta–Trinity National Forest, Platina, CA 96076. (916) 352-4211. A good topographical map is available for purchase.

Length: Variable, a minimum of 2.5 miles one way

Difficulty: Moderate

Starting point: 5,500 feet

High point:
  Pettijohn Trail: 7,100 feet
  Black Rock Lake Trail: 6,300 feet
  North Yolla Bolly Lake Trail: 6,800 feet
  North Yolla Bolly Mountain Trail: 7,900 feet
  Black Rock Mountain Trail: 7,755 feet

Uses: Hiking, horseback riding

Season: June through September

Facilities: Outhouse at trailhead

Water: Available year-round from Black Rock Lake, North Yolla Bolly Lake, and the South Fork Trinity River; many other streams can dry up by late summer

Maps: USGS Yolla Bolly and USGS Black Rock Mountain

The North Yolla Bolly mountains are considered by many to be less beautiful than their geological cousins, the spectacular Trinity Alps and Marble Mountains. Perhaps such a subjective judgment is true for some, but the North Yolla Bolly mountains have much to offer, including high rocky peaks similar to those that make its wilderness-area relatives to the north so justly famous.

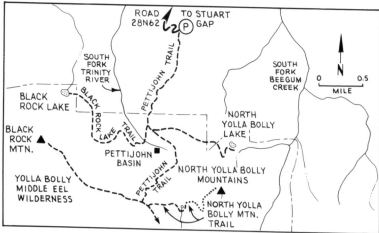

The North Yolla Bolly trails are compactly clustered in the Yolla Bolly Middle Eel Wilderness Area, the southernmost extension of the Klamath mountain range. The trail system described here offers several hiking options. From the central Pettijohn Trail you can choose from four side hikes: Black Rock Lake, North Yolla Bolly Lake, North Yolla Bolly Mountain, and Black Rock Mountain. Since it's difficult to do all four in one day, consider visiting one lake and climbing one peak, options that give you the opportunity to enjoy the seclusion and serenity of an alpine body of water and let you enjoy the spectacular 360-degree view from a mountaintop.

This area is ideal for an overnight backpacking trip, which would allow thorough exploration of the region and the possibility of doing all four side hikes. Good campsites are available in the meadows near the beginning of the Black Rock Lake Trail, at both lakes, and at the spring a few hundred yards along the trail to the North Yolla Bolly Mountain summit. All these sites have year-round water.

From Red Bluff drive 47 miles up Highway 36 to Platina. From Redding, take Clear Creek Road 40 miles from Highway 273 to Platina. From Platina follow Highway 36 west for 11 miles. One-quarter mile past the Hayfork Creek Bridge turn left onto Wildwood–Mad River Road (Road 30). Follow this road about 9 miles to Pine Root Saddle, where you turn left onto Road 35. Follow this road about 10 miles, until you reach an intersection of several roads. A sign saying "Stuart Gap Trailhead" directs you up the last 1.8 miles to the trailhead. All roads are smooth, easy driving, and, except for the last 1.8 miles, paved.

The Pettijohn Trail leaves the parking area and climbs under the shade of firs and pines to meet a long ridge after 2.5 miles. The first mile of this central trail rises relatively gently, but the last 1.5 miles will give you a good workout. The two lake trails branch off about midway up to the ridge, the two peak trails from the ridge's crest. The Pettijohn Trail then connects with the other trails that wind their way through the Mendocino National Forest.

Black Rock Lake Trail. This signed trail leaves the Pettijohn Trail on the right about 1.0 mile from the trailhead. It immediately drops down into Pettijohn Basin, where a large, flower-filled meadow allows a view of the sheer rock face of North Yolla Bolly Mountain. The year-round stream running through the meadow is the South Fork of the Trinity River, which begins its journey to the Pacific Ocean in the mountains above. White fir is the dominant tree species, although you'll also see red fir, incense cedar, and Jeffrey pine. Dense mountain alder thickets grow along the fledgling river.

The trail crosses another stream a few hundred yards later, then undulates through the forest. It fades at times, but tree blazes and small rock stacks will guide you.

One and a half miles from the Pettijohn Trail you'll reach Black Rock Lake. The very shallow water makes swimming difficult, but the surrounding dense forest and the view of the sheer dark face of Black Rock Mountain make the hike more than worth the effort.

North Yolla Bolly Lake Trail. This small lake (about 3 acres) is both more attractive and more secluded than Black Rock Lake. The signed trail leaves the Pettijohn Trail on the left 0.25-mile past the Black Rock Lake Trail turnoff. The path is faint and shows little signs of use, but don't be discouraged: it means that you'll probably have the lake all to yourself.

The trail rises steeply for the first 0.75 mile. At the end of this long climb the trail reaches a ridge. Just to the left, a rock outcropping allows unimpeded views of mountains marching off to the west and north, and the Sacramento Valley stretching out to the Cascades to the east. You'll also see the lake itself and the 1,000-foot-high, gray rock cliff stretching above it. The trail then contours across slippery crumbled rock before dropping down to the lake.

North Yolla Bolly Mountain Trail. Where the Pettijohn Trail crosses the ridge, turn left and follow the trail indicated by the "North Yolla Bolly Station Spring" sign. This trail heads east and briefly follows the ridge before gently descending across loose rock. One-half mile from the trail's beginning you'll enter a small, rock-walled cirque and find a lush little meadow, a campsite, and ice-cold water flowing from a pipe at the mouth of a spring. This spring is the only sure source of water on the ridge.

From here the trail crosses the small creek emanating from the spring, then peters out 200 yards later. Although you'll see remnants of an old unmaintained trail, start climbing straight up (southeast) to the ridge. Once you've gained the ridge, follow it northeast (left) and make your way to the summit. The climb begins in fir trees, but on the ridge itself you'll find mostly foxtail pine, a hardy species that can withstand the extreme weather conditions prevalent on high, exposed ridges.

Once at the top, 1.0 mile from the Pettijohn Trail, you'll realize the difficulty of defining the summit of North Yolla Bolly Mountain. Indeed, some maps use the plural to refer to these heights, for at least three "peaks" share roughly the same elevation (about 7,900 feet). You can decide which is the true summit.

You can obtain the best view by following the ridge to its easternmost point. When the weather's clear you'll see the treeless peaks of the Trinity Alps thrust against the sky to the north, Mount Shasta in isolated grandeur to the northeast, Mount Lassen and the rest of the Cascade Range looming beyond the Sacramento Valley to the east, and the rest of the Yolla Bolly mountains and Coast Range stretching as far as the eye can see to the south and west.

Black Rock Mountain Trail. This signed trail begins at the ridge from the Pettijohn Trail, and offers views to the north and south. It heads right, following the lupine-covered ridge most of the way on its 1.8-mile westward journey to the fire lookout atop 7,755-foot-high Black Rock Mountain, and gains most of its elevation over the last few hundred yards.

Although it's longer than the route to the top of North Yolla Bolly Mountain, the going is significantly easier. The two mountain summits share similar views.

. . . .
55 IDES COVE LOOP TRAIL

Jurisdiction and information: Corning Ranger District, Mendocino National Forest, 22000 Corning Road, Corning, CA 96021. (916) 824-5196. A good topographical map is available for purchase.
Length: 11.0-mile loop
Difficulty: Moderate
Starting point: 6,900 feet
High point: 7,500 feet
Trail characteristics: Narrow, occasionally faint, and composed of small rocks
Uses: Hiking, horseback riding
Season: June to September
Facilities: None
Water: Generally available from lakes, streams, and springs, but may be scarce in late summer
Map: USGS Yolla Bolly

The Ides Cove Loop Trail leads you through lush meadows and pine and fir forest to two small lakes, and gives excellent unobstructed views in all directions. Agile hikers in good shape can also climb 8,092-foot-high Mount Linn, the tallest peak in the Mendocino National Forest. An extensive trail

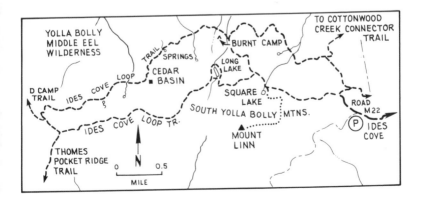

system covers the Yolla Bolly Middle Eel Wilderness Area; you could backpack for a week or longer if you wished. Trails are occasionally faint, so keep your eyes peeled for trail intersections. Hikers who don't want to hike the entire loop, take heart: the best features are located along the first 3.5 miles of trail.

Take A-9 from Corning 20 miles to Paskenta, where you turn right onto Road M2 (23NO1) at the fork. Follow this curvy road 25 miles uphill to Cold Springs Fire Station, then turn right onto Road M22 (25NO1). Stay on M22 for a little over 8 miles to where a sign directs you left for the Ides Cove trailhead. Drive uphill for the last 2.2 miles. The road from Paskenta to the trailhead is paved for the first 20 miles, and is good dirt road thereafter. The last 2.0 miles are a bit rough, but passable. Look out for logging trucks the whole way.

Initially, the trail runs relatively level, with some undulations. After 0.5 mile, the north end of the loop comes in on the right. Continue straight, past some springs. The dominant tree species for this area is red fir, with some Jeffrey pine and western white pine mixed in.

Diminutive Square Lake, elevation 7,000 feet, lies 1.3 miles from the trailhead. At 0.5 acre and only 2 feet deep, you'll probably find its surrounding meadows more attractive. These meadows have been heavily trampled in recent years, and the forest service requests that horses stay out of them.

Mount Linn towers above Square Lake. Surmounting its summit presents a modest challenge that can be met without too much effort or danger. Follow the trail along the east side of the lake, then head east cross-country over to a timbered ridge. Climb south up this ridge until it meets the main, nearly bare, ridge of Mount Linn. Then go west a few hundred yards to the summit, where two government survey markers affirm your successful ascent. Do not head straight up the mountain from the lake: you'll slip and slide much of the way and make a significant contribution to the erosion of the mountain.

Climbing Mount Linn rewards you with excellent views in all directions. To the north, Mount Shasta, the Trinity Alps, and the North Yolla Bollys pierce the skyline. To the east stretches the Sacramento Valley, the Cascades, and the Sierra Nevada. To the south and west the mountains of the Coast Range march serenely to the Pacific Ocean. Hawks will likely soar above you, and observant Clark's nutcrackers will comment on your presence from the shelter of red fir, foxtail pine, and the occasional stunted Jeffrey pine. Although it's possible to hike cross-country to Long Lake from the summit of Mount Linn, it's best to retrace your steps to Square Lake.

The main trail heads 0.3 mile west from Square Lake, where it meets the Burnt Camp Cutoff Trail. If you wish, you can take this trail downhill, thus shortening the loop considerably.

Long Lake, elevation 7,050 feet, 0.9 mile past Square Lake, sits just south of the trail. A small rock pile marks the access trail. Long Lake

A hiker takes a rest at Long Lake.

shares Square Lake's size, depth, and appearance. An encircling trail shows numerous foot-long fish anxiously awaiting a chance to become someone's dinner. Mountain alder crowds the shore, and a forest of Jeffrey pine and red fir surrounds the entire lake.

Continuing along the main trail, you'll cross Long Lake's main tributary where it gushes through a lush meadow. This stream is the last water source for several miles.

The trail then climbs steeply for 1.0 mile to a ridge, which serves as an excellent final destination. This exposed 7,500-foot vantage point offers sweeping vistas similar to those from the top of Mount Linn. Stunted Jeffrey pines, battered by the elements, eke out a precarious existence here. The gray rocks under your feet are Graywacke sandstone, the dominant rock of the southern Yolla Bollys.

To complete the loop trail, which has few broad vistas in its northern section, follow the path down the ridge. After 1.5 dry and exposed miles, the Thomes Pocket Ridge Trail takes off on the left. Go straight, and turn right 300 yards later at the sign directing you to Burnt Camp.

You have now reached the westernmost point of the hike, and will be heading in an easterly direction back to the trailhead. The trail drops 200 feet, then levels off. It passes several springs and small creeks, which water nearby mountain alder and willow thickets. About 2.0 miles from the ridge you'll enter Cedar Basin, a wide drainage with several creeks and numerous incense cedar trees.

One and a half miles past Cedar Basin lies Burnt Camp. Slides Creek flows through a large meadow, and you'll find the camp itself on the west side, by dense thickets of mountain alder. The trail forks here. The Burnt Camp Cutoff Trail on the right climbs steeply 0.8 mile up to the upper trail, just west of Square Lake, and will save you 0.5 mile of walking. The main trail continues east, meeting the Cottonwood Creek Connector Trail 1.5 miles farther. Stay right and ascend another 0.75 mile to where a horse trail comes in on the left. Bear right again, then turn left 300 yards later when you join the main trail. Then drag your weary body the last 0.5 mile to the trailhead.

. . . .

56 SNOW MOUNTAIN TRAIL

Jurisdiction and information: Stonyford Ranger District, Mendocino National Forest, 5080 Ladoga-Stonyford Road, Stonyford, CA 95979. (916) 963-3128. A good topographical map is available for purchase.
Length: 4.0 miles one way
Difficulty: Moderate
Starting point: 5,250 feet
High point: 7,056 feet
Trail characteristics: Generally good, except for rocky areas near the summit
Uses: Hiking, horseback riding
Season: June to September
Facilities: None
Water: None, bring your own
Maps: USGS Stonyford and USGS Pillsbury Lake

The hike to the top of the twin summits of Snow Mountain provides a variety of diverse scenery ranging from exotically colored metamorphic rocks to fir stands to exquisite panoramic views of Northern California. You'll certainly notice the range of color of the rocks and soil. Chert and green-

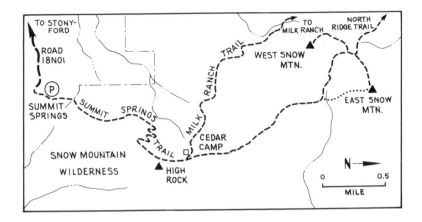

stone create shades of red and green, and in many areas the soil is tinted lavender. The trail itself is signed at all intersections, so you should have no trouble finding your way.

Get to the small town of Stonyford by taking either the Maxwell or Willows exit off I-5. From Stonyford take Road M-10 (18N01) and keep following signs for Summit Springs and Snow Mountain. After driving M-10 about 24 miles from Stonyford, a sign saying "Trailhead 1" will direct you up the last steep 1.4 miles to the trailhead parking area at Summit Springs. The first 12 miles of M-10 are paved. The rest of the way is fairly good dirt and gravel.

As you begin hiking, you'll see much evidence of the 1987 fire that burned the south and west sides of Snow Mountain. Notice how well the vegetation has grown back along the first mile of trail. Still, you'll probably be glad to leave the exposed burn area behind when the trail enters the shaded forest and begins switch backing up to a ridge. As you hike along this ridge you'll have views to the east, west, and south, in addition to the southern flanks of Snow Mountain. Keep your eyes peeled for High Rock, a large outcropping about 300 yards east of the trail. Climbing High Rock gives sweeping views similar to the summits of Snow Mountain, lacking only the northern vista.

The trail eventually leaves the ridge and re-enters the fir forest. After passing some very faint side trails, you'll come to Cedar Camp, where, incidentally, you won't find even a single cedar. The camp, located about 2 miles from the trailhead, borders the edge of a small meadow sporting an even smaller pond. The Milk Ranch Trail leaves from here, and there's a good spring 0.5 mile down it for those in need of water. The main trail, however, continues straight, along the meadow's north edge. After climbing for nearly 0.75 mile, you'll enter the open basin below the twin summits of Snow Mountain, then hike another 0.75 mile up to a saddle.

View of East Snow Mountain from the summit of West Snow Mountain

Three trails leave from this saddle. The middle one, the North Ridge Trail, heads northwest along a green-tinted ridge. It's worth exploring for those who wish to extend their hike.

The trail on the left climbs up to the 7,038-foot-high ridge of West Snow Mountain. From here you'll be delighted by the views of Mount Linn and Mount Shasta to the north, the Sierra Nevada, Sutter Buttes, Sacramento Valley, and Stony Creek Gorge to the east, and row upon row of Coast Range mountains stretching to the south and west. If you look carefully to the southeast, you'll see part of Clear Lake.

After conquering West Snow Mountain you'll no doubt want to cap off your day by climbing East Snow Mountain, 18 feet higher than its sibling. From the above-mentioned saddle, take the right-hand trail and follow it a few hundred yards to the summit. You'll have similar views, with the addition of Mount Lassen. Both summits sport a psychedelic assortment of multicolored rocks and soils.

From near the top of East Snow Peak you can take a cross-country shortcut across the basin back to the main trail you hiked up. There are many other interconnecting trails in the Snow Mountain Wilderness. Those interested in a backpacking trip should contact the ranger station in Stonyford.

CHAPTER EIGHT
. . . .
The Sacramento Valley Floor

The Sacramento River and its many tributary streams have created over the millennia a broad fertile valley bounded by the Coast Range on the west and the Sierra Nevada on the east. This chapter's trails run along the Sacramento River or beside lakes, ponds, or creeks.

Due to the presence of so much water, riparian plant species, such as cottonwoods and willows, dominate the landscape. In addition, hundreds of thousands of water birds make the valley their home. Some, such as

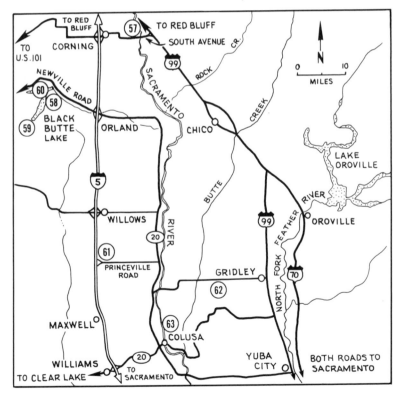

egrets and great blue herons, reside year-round. Others, such as Canada and snow geese, stop in winter as they travel the Pacific flyway from cold northern climes to warm southern regions.

The Woodson Bridge State Recreation Area and the Colusa–Sacramento River State Recreation Area both border the Sacramento River and allow you to hike through the riparian vegetation along the water's edge. The Sacramento National Wildlife Refuge and the Gray Lodge Wildlife Area, which encompass numerous ponds, creeks, and sloughs, offer the highest numbers and greatest species variety of water birds. The Black Butte Lake trails (hikes 59–63) run beside and through the grassy, blue, oak-dotted hills surrounding Black Butte Lake and offer views of the valley floor and the nearby Coast Range.

57 WOODSON BRIDGE STATE RECREATION AREA/TEHAMA COUNTY PARK

Jurisdiction and information: Woodson Bridge State Recreation Area, 25340 South Avenue, Corning, CA 96021. (916) 839-2112.
Length: 1.5 miles of interconnected trails
Difficulty: Easy
Starting point: 100 feet
High point: 100 feet
Trail characteristics: Packed dirt
Uses: Hiking
Season: Year-round
Facilities: 46 campsites (fee required), picnic tables, boat launch; toilets at the campground and at Tehama County Park
Water: Available from drinking fountains
Map: USGS Corning

Though bordering the sights and sounds of civilization, these two adjacent parks offer some pleasant walking, and those so inclined can picnic, fish, or go boating.

However, the flora and fauna are the main attraction. Thick-trunked valley oaks dominate the landscape, their roots firmly embedded in the rich, fertile soil deposited over many thousands of years by the Sacramento River. White alder, cottonwood, and willow are also prevalent in riparian areas, and many trees provide natural trellises for wild grapevines.

Many types of aquatic birds reside here at various times of the year. You can expect to see ducks, geese, and great blue herons, in addition to a wide variety of birds that make their home in the fields and woodlands of the Sacramento Valley. Also, bald eagles often winter here.

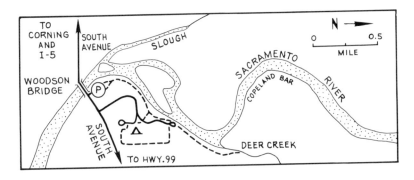

From I-5, take the South Avenue exit near Corning. Follow South Avenue east for 6 miles, then turn at the first left past the bridge. From Highway 99, take the South Avenue turnoff, which is about 15 miles north of Chico. Go west for 3 miles, then take the last right before the bridge.

Two trails leave from the north side of Tehama County Park, and they connect with trails (noted by "nature trail" signs) that wind through the

Hikers explore the lush environs of the Woodson Bridge State Recreation Area.

Woodson Bridge State Recreation Area. An unmarked trail hugs the river bank, thus allowing open views of the cottonwood trees on the west side of the river and the best opportunity to observe aquatic birds. A gravel bar beginning near the bridge also merits exploration.

The north edge of the official hiking territory is bounded by a small picnic area. A private dirt road continues north along the river and is generally open to hikers up to the mouth of Deer Creek, which empties into the river 0.5 mile upstream.

58 EAGLE PASS

Jurisdiction and information: U.S. Army Corps of Engineers, Black Butte Lake, 19225 Newville Road, Orland, CA 95963. (916) 865-4781.
Length: Variable
Difficulty: Moderate
Starting point: 200 feet
High point: 350 feet
Trail characteristics: Cross-country hiking on faint paths, grassy hillsides, and rocky buttes
Uses: Hiking, horseback riding
Season: Year-round
Facilities: Flush toilets at trailhead
Water: Available from fountains at the parking lot
Map: USGS Flournoy

The dark, mysterious Orland Buttes surround Black Butte Lake and give the reservoir its name. Massive basaltic lava flows from the vicinity of Chico and Red Bluff laid down the dark rock approximately 20 million years ago. Stony Creek then slowly eroded weaker sections while depositing clay, silt, sand, and rock.

Besides offering recreational opportunities, such as swimming, picnicking, fishing, boating, and camping, Black Butte Lake controls floods from its main tributary, Stony Creek, and provides irrigation water for local farmers. The dam was completed in 1963, and the lake filled in 1964. East Park Reservoir and Stony Gorge Reservoir, completed in 1910 and 1928, lie farther upstream (south) and serve the same two purposes.

From the main Orland exit off I-5, drive 5.9 miles west on Newville Road, then turn left at the sign for Eagle Pass. Follow the signs for the last mile, then park at the southern lot.

This hike offers the best opportunity to actually get into the buttes. Follow the faint trail straight uphill to the ridge. Here a panoramic 360-degree view unfolds before you: the lake's entire expanse stretches below, wooded foothills march up to the steep slopes of the Coast Range to the west, the broad Sacramento Valley lies east, and distant Mount Shasta and Mount Lassen highlight the mountainous horizon beyond.

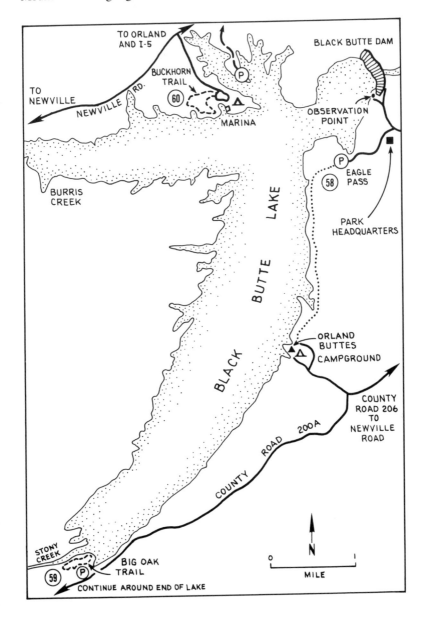

A view of Black Butte Lake and the Orland Buttes rewards those who roam the hills near Eagle Pass.

You can choose to hike southward along the basaltic ridge crest or traverse gentler hillsides closer to the lake. As you head southwest, fences will eventually force you closer to the lake. The Orland Buttes Campground, about a 3-mile hike south, makes a good destination.

59 BIG OAK TRAIL

Jurisdiction and information: U.S. Army Corps of Engineers, Black Butte Lake, 19225 Newville Road, Orland, CA 95963. (916) 865-4781.
Length: 0.8-mile loop
Difficulty: Easy
Starting point: 150 feet
High point: 150 feet
Trail characteristics: Fine dark sand
Uses: Hiking, mountainbiking, horseback riding
Season: Year-round
Facilities: Pit toilet at trailhead
Water: None
Map: USGS Fruto

This interpretive nature trail (pick up brochure at the trailhead) takes you through riparian habitat on the flood plains of Stony Creek. You'll see massive valley oaks and cottonwoods, and pass by willow thickets and buckeye trees. Look for the salt cedar and the lone patch of bamboo: these two plant species aren't native to California. Also note the wide variety of plant life that grows in this area of abundant water and fertile soil. By contrast, the surrounding hills usually support only blue oak, though this is partially due to past periods of heavy animal grazing.

Take the main Orland exit off I-5 and go 5.0 miles west on Newville Road, then turn left onto Road 206. Drive 2.8 miles, then turn left onto Road 200A. Follow this road about 3.5 miles to the unmarked gravel parking lot on the right. The trail begins by the trail sign and brochure holder.

· ·

60 BUCKHORN TRAIL

Jurisdiction and information: U.S. Army Corps of Engineers, Black Butte Lake, 19225 Newville Road, Orland, CA 95963. (916) 865-4781.
Length: 1.3-mile loop
Difficulty: Easy
Starting point: 175 feet
High point: 200 feet
Trail characteristics: Wide dirt path
Uses: Hiking, mountainbiking, horseback riding
Season: Year-round
Facilities: Camping (fee required), flush toilets
Water: Available from fountains in the campground
Map: USGS Flournoy

As with the Big Oak Trail to the south, the Buckhorn Trail has an informative brochure that explains various aspects of local human and natural history. Its proximity to the campground and marina make it less secluded than other possible hikes at the lake, but it does offer open views of the lake and the buttes.

Blue oaks dot the gently sloping hillsides, and you'll have ample opportunity to observe various water birds near the lakeshore. This area is particularly conducive to cross-country hiking, either through the hills or along the edge of the lake.

Take the main Orland exit off I-5 and drive 11.8 miles west on Newville Road, then turn left by the Buckhorn Recreation Area sign. (This road is 0.5 mile past the turnoff for Black Butte Road, which goes to Corning.) Drive into the campground for 1.0 mile, turn right at the first ungated road, then park at the lot on the left. The trail begins on the right.

61 SACRAMENTO NATIONAL WILDLIFE REFUGE

Jurisdiction and information: Sacramento National Wildlife Refuge, 752
  County Road, 99 W, Willows, CA 95988. (916) 934-2801.
Length: 1.0 mile
Difficulty: Easy
Starting point: 90 feet
High point: 90 feet
Trail characteristics: Dirt road
Uses: Hiking
Season: Year-round. Water-bird numbers peak in November and December
Hours open: Sunrise to sunset
Facilities: Bathrooms at the Visitor's Information Center
Water: Available at the Visitor's Information Center
Map: USGS Maxwell

The Wetlands Walk, the only hiking trail on the refuge, isn't the main attraction, but does provide an opportunity for weary I-5 travelers to stretch
their legs. Plans call for extending the trail's length by 1.0 mile and providing an interpretive brochure.

While visitors should certainly hike the Wetlands Walk, the primary reason for coming here is to learn about the myriad water-bird species that
make this area their winter home, and to observe them by taking the
6-mile-long auto tour. A kiosk by the parking lot has informative maps and
brochures, and several signs discuss waterfowl migration routes and other
interesting aspects of the refuge. The Visitor's Information Center, open
daily October through March from 7:30 A.M. until 4:00 P.M., has a wildlife display, a waterfowl video, and also sells nature books.

Take the Norman Road–Princeton exit off I-5 7 miles south of Willows.
Head east, then follow signs to the refuge.

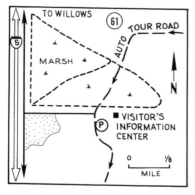
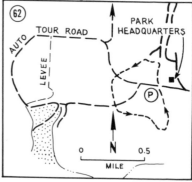

A large flock of snow geese graces both water and sky at the Sacramento National Wildlife Refuge.

The Wetlands Walk, well marked with signs, begins near the Visitor's Information Center. It circles an area of permanent standing water near I-5 and offers opportunities to observe water birds. In addition, you'll see willows, cottonwoods, and a variety of other riparian plants.

The trail forks about 0.3 mile from the Visitor's Information Center. Go left through the middle of the marsh: you'll spend less time near I-5.

Take the auto tour before leaving: you won't be disappointed. The gravel road is in good shape, and takes you back to areas of high water-bird concentration. A trip in late autumn or winter should bring the unforgettable sight of thousands of brilliantly white snow geese circling in the crisp, cool air. A large variety of other water birds will also show themselves, including egrets, great blue herons, Canada geese, avocets, and many species of duck. The refuge is also home to raptors such as red-tailed hawks and barn owls, and to mammals such as raccoons, jackrabbits, and ground squirrels. Be sure to bring your camera: you should get numerous opportunities for great shots.

. . . .

62   GRAY LODGE WILDLIFE AREA

Jurisdiction and information: California State Department of Fish and Game, Gray Lodge Wildlife Area, P.O. Box 37, Gridley, CA 95948. (916) 846-3315 or (916) 846-5176. Excellent brochures are available.

Length: 2.0-mile loop and 3.5-mile auto tour are open year-round. Another 60 miles of roads and levees are open to hikers, except during duck-hunting season (last week in October through the first week in January)

Difficulty: Easy

Starting point: 60 feet

High point: 60 feet

Trail characteristics: Easy walking on dirt roads and levees

Uses: Hiking, biking. Cyclists must follow the rules for hikers

Season: Year-round. Water-bird numbers highest from late October through February

Hours open: Sunrise to sunset

Facilities: Pit toilets at parking lot 14

Water: Available from a fountain by park headquarters near parking lot 14

Map: USGS Butte City

The magic of this place envelops you the first time you see a thousand snow geese fill the sky in a cacophonous, whirling dance of white. The many different species of birds, and their large numbers, make the Gray Lodge Wildlife Area a special place to visit. Located along the Pacific flyway, this part of the Sacramento Valley is a major winter host to the ducks, geese, and other waterfowl that follow the dying autumn south in search of food and tolerable temperatures.

While late fall and winter are the best times to visit, spring and summer still provide much to interest the visitor. Red-winged blackbirds are year-round residents, and flit in and out of cattails and tules at the edges of marshes and ponds. Black-tailed deer, including some albinos, make the area a permanent home, along with owls, hawks, raccoons, ringtails, squirrels, otter, and beaver. Also, the steep slopes of the Sutter Buttes punctuate the southern skyline, their rise made more dramatic by the flatness of the surrounding valley floor.

Take Highway 99 to the town of Gridley, located between Chico and Yuba City. Turn west on Sycamore Street, then left (south) 6 miles later onto Pennington Road. Keep your eyes peeled for Pennington Road; it's easy to miss. To reach the hiking area, take Pennington Road 3 miles south, turn right onto Rutherford Road, then drive the last 2.5 miles to parking lot 14, where you'll have to pay an entrance fee. An alternative route to Pennington Road entails taking the Highway 20 exit off I-5 to Colusa, then crossing the Sacramento River. Follow River Road, which

The Sutter Buttes dominate the skyline at the Gray Lodge Wildlife area.

becomes the Colusa–Gridley Highway. Turn right (south) onto Pennington Road about 6 miles after passing the Butte County line.

There are over 60 miles of roads, trails, and levees open to hikers. During hunting season, which runs from approximately the last week in October through the first week in January, only the 2.0-mile loop trail and 3.5-mile auto-tour route are available.

Discover your own favorite hiking routes. You can come back time and time again and never do the same path twice. For starters, drive the auto-tour route, then park at any of the numerous lots and hike the levees and dirt roads that radiate in all directions. To see the most birds, hike away from the road along open water. Some advice: be prepared for mosquitoes.

The 2.0-mile loop trail begins by the big sign at lot 14. It passes through three main types of habitat: relatively dry upland, which hosts plants and animals often found in the foothills; riparian, where permanent water provides a home for beaver and otter under willows and cottonwoods; and marshland, most of which has been artificially created and is the primary haunt of migrating waterfowl when flooded in winter.

Signs point the way along the entire route of the loop trail, except at two forks within the first 0.5 mile. Go left both times. If it isn't hunting season you'll find several inviting levees to hike on. One of the best heads north just when the trail goes west about 300 yards from lot 14. The loop trail intersects the auto-tour road twice, and you can shorten your walk by taking the road back.

63 COLUSA–SACRAMENTO RIVER STATE RECREATION AREA

Jurisdiction and information: Colusa–Sacramento River State Recreation Area, P.O. Box 207, Colusa, CA 95932. (916) 458-4927.
Length: 1.0-mile loop trail in the state park. Several miles of hiking on the levee by the Sacramento River
Difficulty: Easy
Starting point: 40 feet
High point: 40 feet
Trail characteristics: Ranges from packed dirt to paved to gravel
Uses: Hiking, biking
Season: Year-round
Camping: 20 developed sites
Facilities: Camping (fee required), picnic tables; bathrooms in the state park
Water: Available from fountains in the state park
Map: USGS Colusa

Colusa, filled with old buildings and friendly people, stirs images of a more peaceful, quieter time, a time that seems so increasingly distant in today's modern technological society. Not being located along I-5 helps Colusa preserve its 1920s charm: no fast-food chains or rows of gas stations line the streets.

The hiking possibilities described here won't take you through wild lands untouched by man. You'll hear the town's muffled noise and see numerous signs of human activity. But the combination of the Sacramento

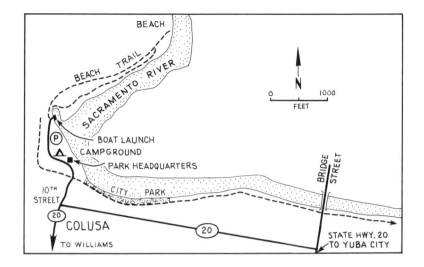

River's scenic beauty, the town's irresistible quaintness, and the wide expanses of fertile farmland make walking here very pleasant.

Take the Highway 20 exit off I-5, then drive 9 miles east to Colusa. Where Highway 20 takes a sharp right turn, go straight on 10th Street into the park. If you only want to hike the levee, park along Highway 20 after the turn, then walk east. The state park has an entrance fee.

The 1.0-mile loop trail begins near a split-rail gate just above the boat launch ramp on the far side of the park. Go either right or left: the two join up 0.5 mile later, just before reaching the river. A vast grove of tall cottonwood trees draped with wild grapevines shades the entire area.

A sandy beach awaits at the river's edge, inviting you to swim the cold waters during summer months. Hiking along the shore in either direction enhances the possibilities of seeing waterfowl and other wildlife.

From the park's southern boundary a levee runs both north and south. South is the best direction for walking. The first 0.8 mile runs through a city park and offers good views of some of Colusa's historic old buildings. The Sutter Buttes loom directly ahead, the Coast Range reigns to the west, and the slow-moving Sacramento River just to the left completes a picturesque scene.

The levee continues for miles beyond the bridge. It passes through some of the most productive agricultural land in the world and provides pastoral views of orchards and farmhouses.

CHAPTER NINE

• • • • • • • • • • •

Chico/Oroville/Paradise Vicinity

Signs of past volcanic activity highlight the hikes in this chapter. The dark basaltic rock that borders Big Chico Creek and Butte Creek are the remains of vast lava flows that covered the region as far back as 50 million years ago.

The North Rim Trail (hike 68), Middle Rim Trail (hike 69), and Yahi Trail (hike 70) in Upper Bidwell Park take you through the Big Chico

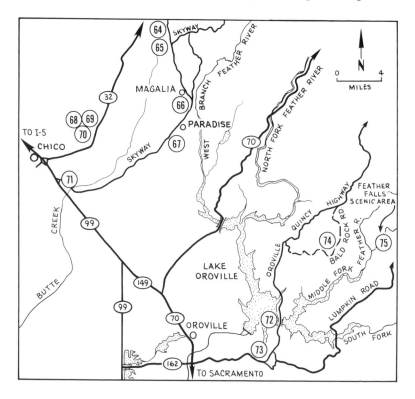

Creek Canyon; the Butte Creek Upper (hike 64) and Lower (hike 65) trails travel through the Butte Creek Canyon; and the Bille Park Trails (hike 67) border the Little Butte Creek Canyon rim. The massive granite batholiths visited by the Bald Rock Trail (hike 74) and the Feather Falls Trail (hike 75) are the remains of vast pools of magma that cooled underground about 80 million years ago and have since been exposed by erosion.

Foothill woodland species, such as digger pine, blue oak, interior live oak, and whiteleaf manzanita, dominate the lower elevation hikes at Upper Bidwell Park (hikes 68, 69, 70) and Lake Oroville (hikes 72, 73). Higher elevation hikes, such as the Upper Ridge Nature Park (hike 66) and Feather Falls (hike 75) trails, take you through the ponderosa pine plant community, where ponderosa pine, Douglas fir, and black oak grow in abundance. At the Chico Tree Improvement Center (hike 71) you'll see a variety of foothill woodland and ponderosa pine plant community species intermixed with exotic trees and shrubs from all over the world.

. . . .

64 BUTTE CREEK UPPER TRAIL

Jurisdiction and information: Bureau of Land Management, 355 Hemsted, Redding, CA 96002. (916) 224-2100.
Length: 1.4 miles one way
Difficulty: Strenuous
Starting point: 2,400 feet
Low point: 2,200 feet
Trail characteristics: Ranges from a wide, flat dirt path to slippery and dangerous rock
Uses: Hiking only
Season: Year-round
Facilities: None
Water: Available from Butte Creek, seasonal creeks, and springs
Map: USGS Paradise

Butte Creek runs from the upper foothills of the Cascades to the Sacramento River, and, in the region you'll hike through, flows down a series of small waterfalls and rapids in between steep, forested mountains. There's good news for those hiking on warm days: swimming holes abound, and immersion in the clear, cool water gives cleansing refreshment. (If swimming is your main goal, a short, 0.3-mile trail heads upstream from the parking area and gives access to several good swimming spots.)

A great variety of vegetation lines the trail. Stands of Douglas fir intermix with ponderosa pine, dogwood, and big-leaf maple. Canyon live oaks cover vast areas of the rugged mountainsides along the creek, with liberal quantities of California laurel mixed in. Ferns and white alders flourish in

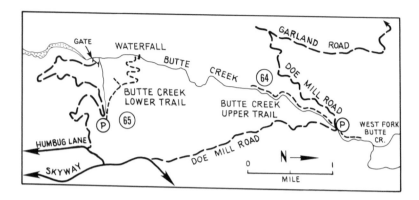

wetter areas.

The trail itself varies to extremes in quality. The first 0.7 mile is relatively easy. However, the way becomes progressively more difficult, with
sections of slippery, faint trail on steep hillsides, and boulders far below
that will cause injury or death to the absentminded and less agile. This trail
is for experienced, attentive hikers who have good hiking shoes. You
shouldn't need climbing equipment or special knowledge, just common
sense and balance.

This trail is definitely not for mountainbikes or horses. One curve on a
steep mountainside is impossible to make on a mountainbike or horse, and
a fall here could easily be fatal.

From Chico, take Highway 32 north for about 20 miles, then turn right
onto Garland Road. Follow this dirt road 2.7 miles, then turn left onto Doe
Mill Road (also dirt). Go 2.0 miles farther to Butte Creek and park on the
west side of the bridge. Alternatively, take the Skyway north from Paradise, then turn left onto Doe Mill Road. Follow this dirt road 2.6 miles to
Butte Creek, and park on the west side of the bridge.

To begin the hike, if you haven't been scared off, follow Doe Mill Road
200 feet uphill from the west side of the bridge. The signed trailhead is on
the left.

After 250 yards, the trail crosses a small creek and enters an active mining claim. One-quarter mile farther it crosses a road, then climbs high
above Butte Creek. A rock outcropping, located on the left about 0.5 mile
from the trailhead, offers great views of the surrounding mountains and the
rushing creek far below. A large intruding rock 0.25 mile past this scenic
lookout necessitates careful navigation.

The trail provides relatively easy hiking for the next 0.3 mile as it undulates above the creek. However, you'll eventually come to areas where the
trail fades or is blocked by fallen trees. Sections of the trail probably extend beyond the 1.4-mile estimate, but it doesn't seem worth the effort of
scrambling over steep, rocky slopes.

65 BUTTE CREEK LOWER TRAIL

Jurisdiction and information: Bureau of Land Management, 355 Hemsted, Redding, CA 96002. (916) 224-2100.
Length: 1.5 miles one way
Difficulty: Moderate
Starting point: 2,250 feet
Low point: 1,500 feet
Trail characteristics: Not good; although relatively easy to follow, the occasionally steep trail is often intruded by scrub oak and fallen trees
Uses: Hiking
Season: Year-round
Facilities: None
Water: Available from Butte Creek, but bring your own
Map: USGS Paradise

This trail is more open to the sun than its sister trail 2.0 miles north (see Butte Creek Upper Trail [hike 64] entry), and involves greater elevation change. It does boast better long-distance views: you'll see the Sutter Buttes and Sacramento Valley to the south, and the Coast Range far in the distance to the west. The Butte Creek Canyon, with its steep, 1,000-foot-high walls, also offers a feast for the eyes.

Take the Paradise exit off Highway 99 in Chico, then follow the Skyway for 20 miles through Paradise and Magalia. Turn left on Humbug Lane, which has large PG&E buildings on both sides. Follow Humbug Lane for 0.3 mile, then turn right onto an unmarked dirt road. Once on the road you should see signs for the Forks of Butte Hydroelectric Project. Follow this dirt road 1.5 miles downhill. The unsigned trailhead begins where the road makes a sharp 180-degree turn. Several large boulders on the edge of the turn make it easier to find. Park near the boulders.

The hike begins on the other side of the little creek that flows by the parking area. Scrub oak borders the trail much of the way, and digger pine, interior live oak, buckbrush, and whiteleaf manzanita are the other major plant species encountered during the dry and sunny first half of the hike.

About 600 yards from the parking area the trail splits after crossing a seasonal creek. Take the upper trail. After continuing downhill another mile the trail passes near a rock outcropping that warrants a detour. The short scramble will reward you with good views of Butte Creek and the surrounding mountains.

As you approach the creek, the vegetation changes to canyon live oak, California laurel, and the occasional big-leaf maple. The alert observer will notice two relatively uncommon trees: California buckeye and California nutmeg. Butte Creek, a large stream that eventually joins the Sacra-

Butte Creek sports numerous swimming holes and small waterfalls.

mento River near the Sutter Buttes, provides beautiful scenery at the point where the trail ends. Rock hop 150 feet upstream and you'll find a great swimming hole, with a 15-foot waterfall just beyond. Several white alder give shade for resting and eating lunch. You'll need the energy to climb back up to the trailhead.

66 UPPER RIDGE NATURE PARK TRAILS

Jurisdiction and information: Bureau of Land Management, 355 Hemsted, Redding, CA 96002. (916) 224-2100.
Length: Up to 2.5 miles total
Difficulty: Easy
Starting point: 2,300 feet
High point: 2,300 feet
Trail characteristics: Wide, flat, leaf- and needle-covered, and easy to walk on
Uses: Hiking, mountainbiking. Horses are allowed only when trails are dry
Season: Year-round
Facilities: None
Water: None
Map: USGS Paradise

The Upper Ridge Nature Park comprises a 120-acre piece of wilderness nestled within the confines of buildings, roads, and other products of civilization. It sports a dense network of interconnected trails well worth thorough exploration.

An impressive diversity of vegetation awaits you. All the major representatives one would expect at this elevation, such as ponderosa pine, Douglas fir, incense cedar, black oak, and whiteleaf manzanita, flourish in abundance, but less common trees like California laurel and madrone also thrive. Interestingly, examples of all ages of species grace this park, not just a mature forest populated mostly by larger, older trees.

Take the Paradise exit off Highway 99 in Chico onto the Skyway. Go north 16.5 miles through the town of Paradise to Magalia, then turn left onto Ponderosa Way. Turn left again on Compton 0.7 mile later, then right onto a gravel road. The trailheads are just down this gravel road near a large sign for the park.

To get yourself oriented, head over from the parking area to a large signboard, which has a trail map of the park. There are two main trails, both with numbered posts. Brochures available in a metal holder explain exactly what is found at each post.

White post numbers distinguish the 0.9-mile-long trail on the east side of the access road. Marked by a hiker symbol, it begins 50 feet north of the signboard. It follows a circular, flat course, and, like all trails here, is well shaded. As with the park's other nature trail, it intersects many unmarked trails that are also good walking.

The trail quickly approaches a school, where you'll hear the joyous sounds of children playing on school days. Don't assume that the nearness of people and houses means there's little wildlife: the author saw five deer. The trail eventually completes a loop, ending back at the signboard.

The 0.8-mile-long trail on the west side of the access road begins just across from the large park sign, and is also marked with a hiker symbol. Its nature interpretation signs have green numbers. It has some gentle ups and downs, and offers a wider variety of plant life and scenery. California laurel emanates a peppery scent, and several big-leaf maples grace the area with their beauty. At post 15 a massive canyon live oak guards a delightful small spring ringed with dogwood.

After passing through an area where tall ponderosa pines and Douglas firs are festooned with wild grapevines hanging from branches as high as 80 feet, the trail crosses the gravel access road, merges with the other trail, then ends at the signboard.

67 BILLE PARK TRAILS

Jurisdiction and information: Paradise Recreation and Parks Department, 6626 Skyway, Paradise, CA 95969. (916) 872-6393.
Length: Varies, up to 1.2 miles total
Difficulty: Easy, for the trails described here
Starting point: 2,050 feet
Low point: 2,000 feet
Trail characteristics: Maintained trail is easy walking; unmaintained trails can be steep, slippery, and intruded by brush
Uses: Hiking
Facilities: Bathrooms in park, playground, picnic tables
Water: Available from drinking fountains
Map: USGS Paradise

Bille Park sits on the east edge of the Little Butte Creek Canyon, and packs a lot of history and nature within its borders. It's a good place to bring the family: picnic, use the playground, then take the kids on the easy self-guided nature walk.

This wooden bridge at Upper Ridge Nature Park spans a small seasonal creek.

From the Skyway in Paradise, turn west onto Bille Road. Go down 0.7 mile, then turn right into the park.

The main trail begins by a fence where a large signboard displays a map of the park and the nature trail. Be sure to grab the nature trail pamphlet. This trail, only 350 feet long, takes you past an old homestead site, a lush spring, and several interesting plant species such as madrone and Scotch broom.

Two trails take off from where the official nature trail ends. The trail to the left goes down 100 yards to a small creek flowing over a steep moss- and lichen-covered rock face—a cool, quiet spot, with the damp smell of verdant plant growth. It's well shaded by white alder and big-leaf maple, and wild grape and blackberry vines grow in abundance.

Leaves and fruit of the blackberry, a common vine found at Bille Park

The trail to the right contours along the hillside, initially under canyon live oaks and California laurel. As it travels the 0.25 mile to an overlook, it goes through a drier area where digger pine, buckbrush, and whiteleaf manzanita predominate.

The overlook is the main highlight of the park. It's easy to believe you've been transported back a thousand years in time: there are few conspicuous signs of civilization visible in any direction. The steep walls of the Little Butte Creek Canyon extend to the north and west, with the far edge of Butte Creek Canyon just beyond. Much farther in the same direction lies the Coast Range. The Sacramento River winds through the valley to the south, and the incongruously placed Sutter Buttes rise conspicuously from the valley floor.

Several faint trails take off from the overlook trail. Feel free to explore these trails, but watch for private property signs. Be prepared for steep, brushy terrain.

68 NORTH RIM TRAIL

Jurisdiction and information: City of Chico Parks Department, 411 Main
   Street, Chico, CA 95927. (916) 895-4972.
Length: 4.8 miles
Difficulty: Moderate
Starting point: 325 feet
High point: 1,325 feet
Trail characteristics: Dirt and basalt rock
Uses: Hiking, mountainbiking, horseback riding
Season: Year-round
Facilities: None
Water: None, bring your own
Maps: USGS Richardson Springs and USGS Paradise

Sweeping views in all directions qualify this hike as the best in Upper Bidwell park. It also wins the most strenuous award, although the old road that serves as the trail gains elevation so gently that you'll hardly believe you've climbed 1,000 feet.

Take the East Avenue exit off Highway 99 in Chico. Head east on East Avenue, which eventually becomes Manzanita Avenue, for about 2.5 miles. A large sign on the left marks the entrance to Upper Bidwell Park. Go 0.9 mile down the main park road from the entrance, then turn left at the sign for the trail and go the last 100 yards to the trailhead.

Follow the dirt road uphill from the parking area as it briefly heads

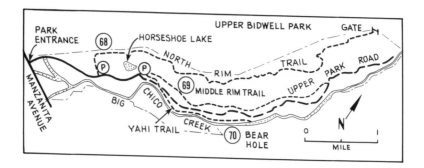

northwest. Once gaining the ridge it turns east and runs past stolid blue oaks and crazily twisted digger pines. Other basalt-rimmed canyons parallel Big Chico Creek's, and you'll see them marching in rows to the north and south. The canyon on your left hosts Sycamore Creek.

However, the most spectacular view lies west. The broad, fertile plains of the Sacramento Valley stretch as far as the eye can see. Just beyond looms the abrupt rise of the Coast Range, which extends clear to the Pacific Ocean.

The last 0.25 mile of trail initially involves a steep, slippery descent past a variety of vegetation, including several members of that peculiar tree tribe, the buckeye. Then, after some relatively mellow walking, your progress along the ridge terminates abruptly. A fence with a locked gate and a "No Trespassing" sign tell you that you've reached the far extent of the park's public land. Forbidden private property lies beyond.

69 MIDDLE RIM TRAIL

Jurisdiction and information: City of Chico Parks Department, 411 Main Street, Chico, CA 95927. (916) 895-4972.
Length: 3.6 miles one way
Difficulty: Easy to moderate
Starting point: 350 feet
High point: 500 feet
Trail characteristics: Dirt and basalt rock
Uses: Hiking, mountainbiking, horseback riding
Season: Year-round
Facilities: None
Water: None, bring your own
Maps: USGS Richardson Springs and USGS Paradise

Three trails, the Upper Rim Trail, the Middle Rim Trail, and the Lower Rim Trail, soon fork from the main trail, then closely parallel each other as they run upstream past digger pine and blue oak. The Lower Rim Trail stays mostly on the flatter ground in the valley floor, while the other two higher trails contour along hillsides, and consequently offer more open views of the valley. Several small trails connect the three. The Upper and Lower Rim trails converge into the Middle Rim Trail about 1.4 miles from the parking area. The Middle Rim Trail then continues its gradual uphill journey, and eventually ends by Upper Park Road.

Blue oaks and buckbrush are sparsely dispersed along all three trails, so there's little shade. However, the open country allows spacious views of the whole canyon, including the steep basaltic rock cap on the rim.

Take the East Avenue exit off Highway 99 in Chico. Head east on East Avenue, which eventually becomes Manzanita Avenue, for about 2.5 miles. A large sign on the left marks the entrance to Upper Bidwell Park. Follow the main park road for 1.6 miles to the unused shooting area just past Horseshoe Lake. Park in the lot on the left. The dirt trail takes off by the road.

70 YAHI TRAIL

Jurisdiction and information: City of Chico Parks Department, 411 Main
   Street, Chico, CA 95927. (916) 895-4972.
Length: 1.5 miles one way
Difficulty: Easy to moderate
Starting point: 300 feet
High point: 400 feet
Trail characteristics: Mostly fine dirt
Uses: Hiking
Season: Year-round
Facilities: None
Water: Available from Big Chico Creek, but bring your own
Maps: USGS Richardson Springs and USGS Paradise

The Yahi Trail, named for the Native Americans that once inhabited this region, offers beautiful close-up views of Big Chico Creek and its accompanying riparian vegetation. Since only hikers are allowed, you'll enjoy the path's offerings in relative solitude. The trail forks in several places, but you'll have little difficulty choosing the right way. Most side trails go down to the creek's edge or to the main road.

Take the East Avenue exit off Highway 99 in Chico. Head east on East

Avenue, which eventually becomes Manzanita Avenue, for about 2.5 miles. A large sign on the left marks the entrance to Upper Bidwell Park. The trail begins on the right side of the park road about 2 miles from the park entrance, and about 200 yards past the point where the pavement ends.

The trail's first mile follows a flat, easy course under the shade of towering sycamores and valley oaks. In this region the creek has reached a more level area and doesn't flow with the same urgency as it does farther up in the canyon's steeper stretches.

Over the last 0.5 mile the trail makes several short though steep ascents and descents, and occasionally enters an old water ditch. Eventually the Yahi Trail becomes a path cut right into the black basalt lining the creek, then ends at the deep, inviting pools of Bear Hole. A faint, intermittent trail continues far upstream along Big Chico Creek's north bank, but it's often steep and intruded by brush.

71 CHICO TREE IMPROVEMENT CENTER NATURE TRAIL

Jurisdiction and information: Chico Tree Improvement Center, Mendocino National Forest, 2741 Cramer Lane, Chico, CA 95928. (916) 895-1176.
Length: 0.6-mile loop nature trail, plus 1.0 mile of roads
Difficulty: Easy
Starting point: 275 feet
High point: 275 feet
Trail characteristics: Paved nature trail; gravel roads
Uses: Hiking
Season: Year-round
Facilities: Picnic tables along the nature trail; no bathrooms at present
Water: Available from a drinking fountain by the main office
Map: USGS Oroville

The Chico Tree Improvement Center encompasses 209 acres and includes dozens of tree species, some native to California, others imported from other countries. The main goal of the center is to produce genetically superior trees, such as ponderosa pine and Douglas fir, that are more resistant to disease, drought, and pollution, then use them for reforestation projects. Spring is the best time to visit: flowers of all hues burst forth from trees, shrubs, and other plants. Autumn is a close second: the leaves of deciduous trees display a variety of reds, oranges, pinks, and yellows.

A hiker signs in for a late afternoon stroll at the Chico Tree Information Center.

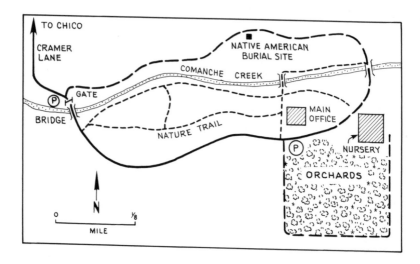

Take the Skyway/Paradise exit off Highway 99 in Chico. Head east (to-wards Paradise) 2 blocks, then turn right onto Zanella Way. Turn left 2 blocks farther onto Morrow Lane. Take the first right off Morrow Lane onto Cramer Lane. Follow Cramer Lane for its 1.0 mile length, then turn left where a large sign welcomes you to the Chico Tree Improvement Center. The road down to the main office is open only from 7:00 A.M. to 4:00 P.M. Monday through Friday. Park just before the gate if you will be hik-ing outside of those hours. Otherwise, continue another 0.4 mile to the large parking lot on the right just across from the main office. The nature trail can be easily accessed from either parking area.

The nature trail travels through a lush forest bordering Comanche Creek, an area planted early in the century with dozens of exotic species. Signs along the trail identify such trees as Chinese cypress, Portuguese cypress, Australian eucalyptus, and many others. Also, look for thick stalks of giant bamboo growing up to 30 feet high near the main office.

Native trees and shrubs are interspersed among the foreign species. Val-ley oaks, cottonwoods, white alders, and digger pines shade willows and blackberries, and wild grapevines intertwine among the branches of many trees, especially near the creek.

Orchards extend both north and south of the nature trail. Two gravel roads travel through these areas, where you'll see groves of pine and fir saplings, in addition to various fruit and nut trees. Feel free to wander among the trees—just don't touch. The northern road passes by the burial site of four Maidu-tribe Native Americans (described in detail on an histor-ical marker) and offers views of the Sierra foothills to the northeast.

72 KELLY RIDGE TRAIL/CHAPARRAL TRAIL

Jurisdiction and information: Lake Oroville State Recreation Area, 400 Glen Drive, Oroville, CA 95966. (916) 538-2200.
Length: 2.7-mile loop
Difficulty: Easy to moderate
Starting point: 1,200 feet
Low point: 900 feet
Trail characteristics: Wide dirt path
Uses: Hiking, horseback riding
Season: Year-round
Facilities: Bathrooms at Visitor's Information Center at the trailhead
Water: Available from fountains at the Visitor's Information Center at the trailhead
Map: USGS Big Bend Mountain

This hike offers two major attractions. The first is the opportunity to learn the major tree and shrub species of the region by hiking the 0.2-mile-long Chaparral Trail (an interpretive nature trail). The second is the panoramic views of the lake and surrounding mountains from the vantage point of Kelly Ridge Point. All trail intersections are signed.

From Highway 70 in Oroville, take the Oroville Dam Boulevard exit and head northeast. Turn right after 1.5 miles onto the Olive Highway. Follow this road for 5 miles, then turn left onto Kelly Ridge Road, where you'll see a large sign for the Lake Oroville State Recreation Area. Follow Kelly Ridge Road 2.0 miles to the Visitor's Information Center. The gate is locked daily at 5:00 P.M., so park outside if you will be hiking later than this time.

To begin, descend the stairs from the Visitor's Information Center, which has information about swimming, fishing, boating, and camping at Lake Oroville. Pick up the Chaparral Trail brochure along the way. You'll immediately come to a fork in the trail: go right. (The trail to the left heads down past the dam and ends 8.0 miles farther near the Feather River just north of Oroville. While some sections of the trail offer good hiking, others pass by houses and near major roads, and several unsigned trail forks and intersections with dirt roads can make navigation difficult.)

After passing by several of the Chaparral Trail's numbered posts, you'll reach a three-way fork in the trail 200 yards from the trailhead. The Chaparral Trail heads right and ends at the Visitor's Information Center parking lot. Hike this section at the end of the loop after you've been to Kelly Ridge Point.

Take the left fork towards Kelly Ridge Point. Keep your eyes peeled for a brief glimpse of Bald Rock's granite dome (hike 74) 10 miles to the northeast. As you gradually descend, notice the surrounding vegetation. It's primarily composed of typical foothill woodland species: whiteleaf manzanita, toyon, buckbrush, interior live oak, blue oak, and digger pine.

A spur trail lies 1.0 mile from the trailhead. Head left on this trail 250 yards to the hike's major destination: Kelly Point Ridge. From here you have open views of the lake and the surrounding mountains. Massive, earth-filled Oroville Dam, completed in 1967, looms 1.5 miles to the west. Lake Oroville provides water for homes, businesses, and agriculture throughout much of the state, including the Bay Area, Central Valley, and Southern California.

To the north stretches the North Fork Feather River arm of the lake, and to the east lies the Highway 162 bridge, which spans the confluence of the Middle Fork Feather River and South Fork Feather River arms.

After savoring this sumptuous view, head back to the main trail and take the left fork. The path climbs gently over the next mile and occasionally allows eastward views of the lake and mountains. A trail fork lies 1.0 mile from Kelly Ridge Point. Turn right and hike the last 0.5 mile back to the Visitor's Information Center. (If you continue straight, you'll eventually reach Saddle Dam and the Roy Rogers/Loafer Creek Loop [hike 73] trailhead after a 2.0-mile jaunt near paved roads, the Bidwell Canyon Campground, and dozens of houses.) Be sure to complete the last section of the Chaparral Trail, which takes off on the left after 0.3 mile.

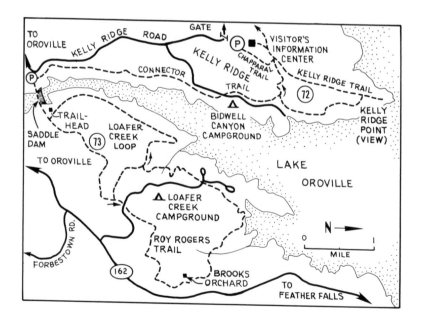

A view of a drought-depleted Lake Oroville from the Roy Rogers Trail

73 LOAFER CREEK LOOP/ROY ROGERS TRAIL

Jurisdiction and information: Lake Oroville State Recreation Area, 400 Glen
   Drive, Oroville, CA 95966. (916) 538-2200.
Length: 4.7-mile loop
Difficulty: Moderate
Starting point: 800 feet
High point: 1,000 feet
Trail characteristics: Dirt path is mostly wide and easy to follow, though oc-
   casionally bordered by poison oak
Uses: Hiking, horseback riding
Season: Year-round
Facilities: Bathrooms at Loafer Creek Campground; outhouses at Brooks
   Orchard
Water: Bring your own
Map: USGS Big Bend Mountain

This combination of two trails passes through a variety of natural and human areas. You'll encounter regions of tall pines and dense oaks, and also
briefly travel by a campground. However, most of the hiking takes place

far from the noise of surrounding civilization: only the occasional sound of a car on the Olive Highway or a boat on the lake will impinge upon your ears.

Take the Oroville Dam Boulevard exit off Highway 70 in Oroville and head northeast. Turn right after 1.5 miles onto the Olive Highway. Follow this road for 5 miles, then turn left onto Kelly Ridge Road, where you'll see a large sign for the Lake Oroville State Recreation Area. Drive 0.5 mile up Kelly Ridge Road and turn right on the dirt road past the "Miner's Ranch Water Treatment Plant" sign. Park off this road near the small dam.

From where you've parked, head east to the dam. (You may notice a trail on the left, which goes 2.0 miles up to the Visitor's Information Center. This isn't your trail.)

The trailhead lies 0.25 mile away on the dam's far side. Here you'll see two posts giving destinations and distances. All trail intersections have similar informational posts, so staying on the right path isn't difficult.

Follow the direction indicated for "Brooks Orchard." The broad trail climbs gently for the first 0.7 mile, passing through typical foothill woodland vegetation: blue oaks, interior live oaks, and digger pines shade toyon, whiteleaf manzanita, and coffee berry.

You'll reach a trail fork about 1.0 mile from the trail head. If you wish to shorten your hike, turn left and follow the Loafer Creek Loop Trail as it circles back to the trailhead. The total hiking distance for this option is 2.0 miles.

Take the right fork to continue the longer Roy Rogers Loop Trail. The trail gently undulates for 1.0 mile, then enters Brooks Orchard. The grassy meadow, horse-watering tank, hitching posts, and picnic tables make this a popular spot for the many equestrians who ride the Lake Oroville trails. Hikers will also enjoy the chance to sit and rest.

The trail crosses a small stream 0.3 mile past Brooks Orchard, then joins an old water ditch built in the 1850s to bring water to a nearby gold mine. After a few hundred yards the trail leaves the water ditch, then approaches the lake. Several small trails go down to the shore, where you'll have the first open views of the lake and surrounding mountains. The water offers an opportunity to cool off on hot days.

The trail then passes by the Loafer Creek Campground, then begins climbing. About 1.5 miles past Brooks Orchard you'll reach a small seasonal creek. Note the change in vegetation in this area: ponderosa pine, black oak, canyon live oak, and buckeye dominate. These species typically grow at higher elevations, but thrive here because the north-facing slope receives less sunlight, thus simulating the cooler conditions found higher up.

The Loafer Creek Loop Trail meets your trail 0.25 mile past the creek: head right. After 0.5 mile the path travels along an open grassy ridge covered with wildflowers in spring, then gently drops down over the next 0.5 mile to the trailhead.

Giant granite boulders near the summit of Bald Rock

74 BALD ROCK TRAIL

Jurisdiction and information: Oroville Ranger District, Plumas National Forest, 875 Mitchell Avenue, Oroville, CA 95965. (916) 534-6500.
Length: Variable, up to 2.0 miles total
Difficulty: Moderate
Starting point: 3,100 feet
High point: 3,350 feet
Trail characteristics: First 0.25 mile is easy walking; no trail on top, but walking on the granite presents little difficulty
Uses: Hiking
Season: Year-round
Facilities: None
Water: Small seasonal creek, bring your own
Map: USGS Big Bend Mountain

Bald Rock began millions of years ago as an underground swelling of hot magma. Over the aeons this magma slowly cooled to form granite. Erosion

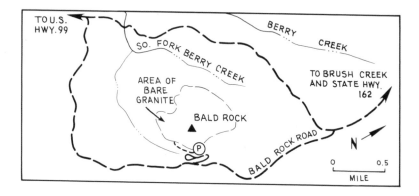

eventually exposed the bare rock from which this prominent feature gains its name.

Take the Oroville Dam Boulevard exit off Highway 70 in Oroville, then head northeast. Turn right after 1.5 miles onto the Olive Highway. Five miles farther head north (left) onto the Oroville Quincy Highway (Highway 162). After 20 miles turn right at Brush Creek onto the dirt road. One and a half miles farther turn right onto Bald Rock Road. About 2 miles farther go straight at the 3-way intersection. One and a third miles from this intersection, as Bald Rock Road is curving to the left, an unsigned dirt road appears on the right-hand side, heading in almost the opposite direction to that in which you are now traveling. Follow this road down 150 feet to the parking area, where it ends in a loop. Pay close attention: this last road is not easy to find, and there are other dirt roads in the area that can mislead you.

Ample rewards repay the struggle to find the trailhead. There isn't much actual trail, but once on top of Bald Rock you can wander where you will.

The trail begins between an incense cedar tree and a dogwood tree at the west side of the parking lot, and for most of its 0.25-mile length it follows a seasonal creek. If you see foot-long cones on the ground, they came from the sugar pines towering high above you.

Once the trail ends it's easy to see the way to the top: just keep climbing up the granite, picking and choosing the best way. Make sure you note where the trail ends so you can easily find it when it's time to return to the trailhead.

Bald Rock offers magnificent views in all directions. The tree-covered mountains of Plumas National Forest surround it, and the fertile fields of the Sacramento Valley lie to the west. As you wander around the 200 or so exposed acres of granite, you'll get a close-up look at nearby terrain. Be careful of your footing; sometimes slippery grains of decomposed granite can be hard to see when walking on sloping rock.

75 FEATHER FALLS TRAIL

Jurisdiction and information: Oroville Ranger District, 875 Mitchell
  Avenue, Oroville, CA 95965. (916) 534-6500.
Length: 3.8 miles one way
Difficulty: Moderate
Starting point: 2,400 feet
Low point: 1,500 feet
Trail characteristics: Well-maintained dirt path makes for easy walking; safety
  rails provided in dangerous areas
Uses: Hiking, mountainbiking (10 mph limit), horseback riding
Season: Year-round. Spring is best for high water flow over the falls, Autumn
  has pretty foliage.
Facilities: Pit toilets at the trailhead
Water: Available from Frey Creek and Fall River. You'll need plenty.
Map: USGS Big Bend Mountain

This hike is one of the book's best. Spectacular Feather Falls, the sixth
highest in the United States at 640 feet, is itself well worth the walk. But
the well-shaded trail to the falls delights the senses as it passes through
stands of towering ponderosa pine and incense cedar, and borders the
clear, rushing waters of Frey Creek. The trail is most beautiful in autumn
when the leaves of dogwood, black oak, and big-leaf maple trees turn to
crimson, yellow, and soft pink.

Take the Oroville Dam Boulevard exit off Highway 70 in Oroville, then
head northeast. Turn right after 1.5 miles onto the Olive Highway. From
here on signs direct you to the falls. Follow the Olive Highway about 6
miles, then turn right onto Forbestown Road. Six miles farther turn left
onto Lumpkin Road, then left again 10 miles farther for the final road to
the trailhead. All roads are paved.

Madrone trees, with their shiny green leaves and reddish peeling bark,
line the first few hundred feet of the trail. It's rare to find so many of this
species in one place, and their presence is an omen of good things to come.
Several California nutmeg trees, also less common forest inhabitants, grow
near the wooden 0.5-mile marker. To identify this tree, gently feel the tips
of the dark green needles—they're surprisingly sharp.

As the trail descends you'll hear the sound of gurgling water, and a bit
past the 1.0-mile marker you'll cross Frey Creek just above its intersection
with Bryant Ravine Creek. The temperature here is the lowest of any part
of the hike: you're deep in a ravine under the shade of maple and alder, and
the cold water and lack of sunlight combine to cool the air.

Pay attention to Frey Creek on your left as you continue: 0.25 mile from
the bridge a small two-stage waterfall with a great swimming hole will

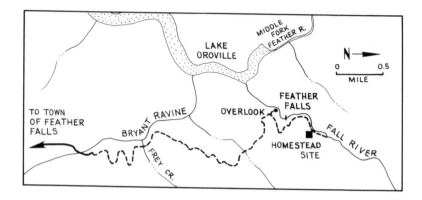

tempt you on hot summer days. Getting down to the creek isn't easy, so be careful and try to prevent erosion from your footsteps.

At the 1.5-mile marker an open space in the trees allows the first good views of the Middle Fork of the Feather River and the sheer granite walls of its canyon. Bald Rock Dome, unmistakably evident on the northwest side, reigns supreme over the entire scene.

The trail continues its generally downhill course for a little more than 1.0 mile, then crosses a lush ravine. From here, the way is uphill, though not steeply. After crossing the ridge, the trail forks at the point where safety railings begin. Follow along the railings, keeping in mind that you are near cliffs. Watch children closely.

Your ears will guide you in the direction of the falls. Hold back the urge to stop and gaze at the view, and continue on 200 yards to another trail fork. Turn left and walk down to the overlook.

Now Feather Falls emerges in all its splendor. With a vertical drop of 640 feet, the water plummets to the gorge below, where much of it vaporizes to a fine mist. Plan to spend a lot of time here; you won't be able to tear your eyes away.

Most of the rock around you is the remains of a granite batholith, a huge mass of molten magma that cooled beneath the earth's surface. As it cooled a fissure formed, and over the millennia Fall River eroded the crack back to the present point of the falls, where it encountered more resistant rock.

Don't become too mesmerized by the falls. Turn around and look at the Fall River gorge, then follow its course with your eyes to where it meets the Middle Fork of the Feather River. Shortly thereafter this magnificent stream meets an ignominious end at Lake Oroville. The same granite walls seen from the viewpoint at the trail's 1.5-mile mark are more easily visible here. Also watch for bald eagles. If you're lucky, they'll fly near and show off their magnificent plumage.

For a close-up view of the falls, head back up to the trail, then go left. After four hundred yards a small trail drops down to Fall River. From

The waters of Feather Falls descend 640 feet beside a sheer granite cliff.

there, scramble over granite boulders to the lip of the falls, where a chain-link fence prevents you from joining the water on its downward course. If you get on your tippytoes in a corner of the fence, you can see the entire length of the falls from a perspective that you will never forget. Be careful in this area, and certainly don't go swimming.

The main trail continues upstream along Fall River for another mile before petering out. On the way it passes an old homestead site, evidenced by apple and walnut trees and the remains of a water ditch. Several swimming areas and campsites are located near the trail, making this area an excellent backpacking destination.

APPENDIX ONE
. . . .
Trails for Mountainbikes

Read the trail description before deciding if this is a good ride for you. Also, rules regarding the use of mountainbikes on these trails may have changed since this book has gone to press. Call the trail's information number if you have any questions.

Chapter 2: Shasta Lake National Recreation Area

12. Centimudi Trail/Shasta Dam
13. Dry Fork Trail
14. Clikapudi Trail
15. Waters Gulch Trails
16. Bailey Cove Trail
18. Hirz Bay Trail
19. Samwel Cave Nature Trail

Chapter 3: Whiskeytown National Recreation Area

21. Great Water Ditch Trail North
22. Camden Water Ditch Trail to El Dorado Mine
24. Clear Creek Vista Trail
25. Boulder Creek Trail
26. Mount Shasta Mine Loop Trail
27. Great Water Ditch Trail South
28. Clear Creek Trail
30. Lower Brandy Creek Trail
31. Upper Brandy Creek Trails

Chapter 5: Hat Creek and Pit River Trails in the Vicinity of Highway 299

Chapter 6: Redding/Anderson/Red Bluff Vicinity

Chapter 8: The Sacramento Valley Floor

Chapter 9: Chico/Oroville/Paradise Vicinity

APPENDIX TWO
· · · · · · · · · · · ·
Trails for Horses

Read the trail description before deciding if this is a good ride for you. Also, rules regarding the use of horses on these trails may have changed since this book has gone to press. Call the trail's information number if you have any questions.

Chapter 1: Castle Crags State Park and Vicinity

9. Pacific Crest Trail
10. Burstarse Falls
11. Twin Lakes/Tamarack Lake Trail

Chapter 2: Shasta Lake National Recreation Area

13. Dry Fork Trail
14. Clikapudi Trail
15. Waters Gulch Trails
16. Bailey Cove Trail
18. Hirz Bay Trail
19. Samwel Cave Nature Trail

Chapter 3: Whiskeytown National Recreation Area

22. Camden Water Ditch Trail to El Dorado Mine
23. Mill Creek Trail
24. Clear Creek Vista Trail
25. Boulder Creek Trail
26. Mount Shasta Mine Loop Trail
27. Great Water Ditch Trail South

Chapter 6: Redding/Anderson/Red Bluff Vicinity

Chapter 7: The Yolla Bollys and the Coast Range

Chapter 8: The Sacramento Valley Floor

Chapter 9: Chico/Oroville/Paradise Vicinity

APPENDIX THREE
Trails for Young Children

Chapter 1: Castle Crags State Park and Vicinity

1. Indian Creek Trail
2. Flume Trail
4. Milt Kenny Trail
6. Castle Dome Trail
7. Root Creek Trail

Chapter 2: Shasta Lake National Recreation Area

12. Centimudi Trail/Shasta Dam
18. Hirz Bay Trail

Chapter 3: Whiskeytown National Recreation Area

21. Great Water Ditch Trail North
22. Camden Water Ditch Trail to El Dorado Mine

Chapter 4: McArthur–Burney Falls Memorial State Park

32. Falls Trail
33. P.S.E.A. Trail
35. Headwaters Trail
36. Pioneer Cemetery Trail

Chapter 5: Hat Creek and Pit River Trails in the Vicinity of Highway 299

Chapter 6: Redding/Anderson/Red Bluff Vicinity

Chapter 8: The Sacramento Valley Floor

Chapter 9: Chico/Oroville/Paradise Vicinity

APPENDIX FOUR

Further Reading

Alt, David D., and Donald W. Hyndman. *Roadside Geology of Northern California*. Missoula, Montana: Mountain Press, 1975.

Hogue, Helen. *Wintu Trails*. Revised edition. Redding, California: Shasta Historical Society, 1977.

Lawson, John D. *Redding and Shasta County: Gateway to the Cascades*. Northridge, California: Windsor Publications, 1986.

Norris, Robert M., and Robert W. Webb. *Geology of California*. 2nd edition. New York: Wiley and Sons, 1990.

Storer, Tracy I., and Robert L. Usinger. *Sierra Nevada Natural History*. Berkeley: University of California Press, 1963.

Whitney, Stephen. *A Sierra Club Naturalist's Guide*. San Francisco: Sierra Club Books, 1979.

Whitney, Stephen. *Western Forests*. New York: Knopf, 1985.

Also, see the Audubon Society field guides and the Peterson field guides. These two series of books give in-depth coverage of plants, animals, and geology.

Index

JOHN R. SOARES was born near Redding, California, and hiked the surrounding hills and mountains of the Sacramento Valley during his youth. His interest in life sciences and biochemistry led to studies in California, Sweden, and New York, and, thus bitten by the travel bug, he hiked extensively through Europe, the Middle East, and North Africa. With a new appreciation for history and politics, Soares returned to the Sacramento Valley, and now teaches political science at two community colleges. His love of exploring and writing were the inspiration for his first book.